HANDBOOK (

The Ultimate Beginner book to use ChatGPT Effectively, Automating Boring Tasks, and Increasing Your Productivity 10x

(New Edition 2023)

ARSATH NATHEEM S

Copyright © 2023 by ARSATH NATHEEM S

All rights Reserved. 2023 Edition

ISBN: 9798378940134

Imprint: Independently published

Author: Arsath Natheem S

This ChatGPT handbook is geared towards providing exact and reliable data with respect to the subject and issue covered. The publication is sold with the idea that the publisher doesn't have to make any qualified services or do anything else.

No way is it okay to copy, print, or share any part of this book, either in digital e-book (eBook) format or on paper. It is against the law to re-document this textbook, and you can't keep this manuscript unless the publisher gives you written permission to do so. All rights reserved.

The respective authors own all rights not held by the publisher. The attributes that are used are without any consent, and the book of the trademark is without permission or backing by the brand owner. All trademarks and brands within this book are for descriptive purposes only and are the owned by the owners themselves, not associated with this textbook

WHY I WROTE THIS BOOK

As the world continues to embrace technology and artificial intelligence, ChatGPT has emerged as a game-changer in the conversational AI space. With over one million registered users in a matter of days, ChatGPT has taken the world by storm, outpacing the growth of popular platforms like Facebook, Netflix, and even the iPhone. This is why I have written the "Handbook of ChatGPT: The Ultimate Beginner's Guide to Using ChatGPT Effectively, Automating Boring Tasks, and Increasing Your Productivity 10x". This book provides a comprehensive guide on how to effectively utilize ChatGPT, a powerful chatbot that can automate repetitive and boring tasks, freeing up your time and allowing you to focus on more important tasks. With ChatGPT, you can access information and support on a wide range of subjects, from science and history to literature and more. It can even help you improve your vocabulary, explain complex concepts, and provide advice and guidance on personal and professional development.

ChatGPT is truly a marvel of technology, with the ability to remember the flow of your conversation and provide relevant answers based on previous interactions. It is not yet advanced enough to replace all human interaction, but it can provide creative and authoritative answers in areas where there is ample training data.

In this book, I aim to provide a comprehensive guide on how to harness the full potential of ChatGPT, automating tedious tasks and boosting your productivity 10x. Whether you're a seasoned tech user or a beginner, the "Handbook of ChatGPT" is a must-read for anyone looking to take advantage of this powerful tool.

"Tell me and I forget, teach me and I may remember, involve me and I learn" — Benjamin Franklin

WHY YOU SHOULD READ THIS BOOK

Are you ready to take your productivity to the next level?

Look no further than "The HANDBOOK OF CHATGPT" - the ultimate guide to mastering the groundbreaking language model created by OpenAI. This book provides a comprehensive and beginner-friendly approach to using ChatGPT to automate tedious tasks, increase productivity, and achieve your goals with ease. Discover how to unlock the full potential of ChatGPT for personal and professional growth with real-world examples and a step-by-step guide to getting started, including accessing the OpenAI API and GPT-3 Playground, training your own models, and fine-tuning models for specific tasks. Take your skills to the next level with advanced features such as language translation, text summarization, and incorporating ChatGPT into various applications and systems.

But that's not all - this book also covers tips for optimizing productivity, including automated content creation, fine-tuning models, and using ChatGPT in workflow automation. Don't let tedious tasks hold you back from achieving your full potential. With "The HANDBOOK OF CHATGPT", you can save time and increase your productivity tenfold. Don't miss out on the opportunity to master this remarkable AI technology and see how it can help you reach new heights of success. Whether you're a student, professional, or entrepreneur, this book is a must-read for anyone looking to achieve more than they ever thought possible. Start your journey towards increased productivity and success today with "The HANDBOOK OF CHATGPT".

It is my sincere hope that you will find this book helpful in creating your story. Best wishes!

TABLE OF CONTENTS

CHAPTER 1 1

INTRODUCTION TO CHATGPT 1

    Introduction: 1

    Overview of ChatGPT and its capabilities 1

    History of ChatGPT 2

    GPT-3 3

    Why ChatGPT is Important 4

    How ChatGPT works 6

    Why isn't ChatGPT is Not Connected to the Internet 7

    What does it mean that Chat GPT is based on transformers? 7

    ChatGPT FAQ (Commonly asked questions about ChatGPT) 9

    Summary: 12

CHAPTER 2 13

GETTING STARTED WITH CHATGPT 13

    How to use ChatGPT Step-by-Step Guide: 13

    How to Register for a ChatGPT Account 14

        Step 1. Go to Chat GPT on Open AI and click "Sign up." 14

        Step 2. Add your email address and create a password. 15

        Step 3. Verify your Email Address. 16

        Step 4. Fill in your personal information 17

        Step 5. Verify your Mobile Number & Start using Chat GPT. 17

        Step 6. Start interacting with ChatGPT 19

    What is ChatGPT prompt? 23

    How GPT prompts work 23

    Prompt Engineering 26

    Social media's Trending ChatGPT example 27

    Who will win in the Google vs. ChatGPT battle? 42

    Interesting Things in ChatGPT 44

    Final Thoughts 44

CHAPTER 3 45

OPENAI CHATGPT-3 PLAYGROUND 45

    Introduction 45

    How to use GPT-3 Playground: 45

Step 1: Visit the OpenAI Playground website 45
Step 2: Create an OpenAI account 46
Step 3: Select the ChatGPT model 46
Step 4: Type a prompt 46
Step 5: Get a response 46
Step 6: Explore additional features 46
Start With a Prompt 47
Try These Fun Prompts 47
Where to View Your Usage 48
Choosing a Different Model 49
Fine-Tuning the Results 49
OpenAI Playground: Accessible to All 50
ChatGPT Playground Examples 50
    1. [Q&A] 51
    2. [Grammar correction] 51
    3. [Summarize for a 2nd grader] 52
    4. [Natural language to OpenAI API] 53
    5. [Text to command] 54
    6. [English to other languages] 54
    7. [Natural language to Stripe API] 55
    8. [SQL translates] 55
    9. [Parse unstructured data] 56
    10. [Classification] 57
    11. [Python to natural language] 58
    12. [Movie to Emoji] 58
    13. [Calculate Time Complexity] 59
    14. [Translate programming languages] 59
    15. [Advanced tweet classifier] 60
    16. [Explain code] 61
    17. [Keywords] 62
    18. [Factual answering] 63
    19. [Ad from product description] 64
    20. [Product name generator] 65
    21. [TL; DR summarization] 65

22. [Python bug fixer] 66
23. [Spreadsheet creator] 67
24. [JavaScript helper chatbot] 68
25. [ML/AI language model tutor] 68
26. [Science fiction book list maker] 69
27. [Tweet classifier] 70
28. [Airport code extractor] 70
29. [SQL request] 71
30. [Extract contact information] 71
31. [JavaScript to Python] 72
32. [Friend chat] 73
33. [Mood to color] 73
34. [Write a Python docstring] 74
35. [Analogy maker] 75
36. [JavaScript one line function] 75
37. [Micro horror story creator] 76
38. [Third-person converter] 76
39. [Notes to summary] 77
40. [VR fitness idea generator] 77
41. [Essay outline] 78
42. [Recipe creator (eat at your own risk)] 79
43. [Chat] 80
44. [Marv the sarcastic chat bot] 80
45. [Turn by turn directions] 81
46. [Restaurant review creator] 82
47. [Create study notes] 82
48. [Interview questions] 83
Summary: 84
CHAPTER 4 85
THE TECHNICAL ASPECTS OF GETTING STARTED 85
Introduction: 85
(1) OpenAI API: 85
(2) OpenAI GPT-3 Playground: 87
(3) Training your own model: 88

- (4) Using pre-trained models: 90
- (5) OpenAI's GPT-3 fine-tuning: 91
- (6) Setting up ChatGPT (e.g., installing necessary libraries, creating an account) 93
- Basic usage of ChatGPT (e.g., inputting text, generating responses) 93
- Understanding the basic input and output format... 94
- Advanced Features of ChatGPT 94
  - Fine-tuning ChatGPT for specific tasks 94
  - Language Translation 94
  - Text Summarization 95
- Using pre-trained models 96
  - Pre-trained models for different languages: 97
  - Pre-trained models for different domains... 97
- Incorporating ChatGPT into applications and systems 98
- How to generate text using the API 99
- Advanced Text Generation with ChatGPT 100
- Fine-tuning models for specific tasks... 101
- Using ChatGPT for automated content creation... 103
  - (1) Blog post generation.. 103
  - (2) Chatbot development... 104
- Best practices for fine-tuning and using ChatGPT... 105
- Here are 5 ways ChatGPT can increase your productivity 106
  - (1) Automating repetitive tasks with ChatGPT (e.g. customer service, data entry) 106
  - (2) How ChatGPT can be used to automate repetitive tasks... 108
  - (3) Using ChatGPT in workflow automation.. 109
  - (4) Examples of real-world productivity applications.. 109
  - (5) Utilizing ChatGPT for brainstorming and idea generation 110
- CHAPTER 5 112
- INCREASING PRODUCTIVITY WITH CHATGPT 112
  - Introduction.. 112
  - Using ChatGPT for text generation (e.g., writing emails, reports) 112
  - Basic Text Generation with ChatGPT 114
    - Understanding the different modes of text generation 114
    - (1) Conditional text generation 114
    - (2) Unconditional text generation 115

Almost Every Business Can Benefit from ChatGPT 115

Enhance your productivity with ChatGPT Chrome extensions 116

    1. WebChatGPT 116

    2. ChatGPT Writer 117

    3. ChatGPT for Google 117

    4. Merlin, an OpenAI ChatGPT-powered personal assistant 117

    5. LINER: ChatGPT Google Assistant & Highlighter 118

    6. TweetGPT 119

    7. YouTube Summary with ChatGPT 119

    8. ChatGPT Prompt Genius 120

    9. Promptheus 120

    10. Summarize 121

    11. Fancy GPT 121

    12. ChatGPT integration with Microsoft Word 122

    13. ChatGPT with Google Sheets and Excel 123

Learning how to use ChatGPT effectively: A lesson in generative AI 124

Use ChatGPT and Midjourney's powerful generative AI tools to create a visually stunning and captivating story. 130

50 ways to make money with ChatGPT 139

CHAPTER 6 142

CHATGPT ALTERNATIVES AND ITS USE CASES 142

    Google Bard 142

    Microsoft Bing 143

    Chatsonic 144

    Jasper Chat 145

    Character AI 146

    You.com 147

    OpenAI Playground 149

    DialoGPT 149

    Perplexity AI 150

    Replika 151

    Neeva AI 152

    Other AI Tools You Should Try Out 153

        Tome 153

        Rytr 154

Socratic AI 155
PepperType 156
CHAPTER 7 158
TROUBLESHOOTING AND MAINTENANCE 158
Introduction: 158
Common issues with ChatGPT and how to resolve them 159
Tips for maintaining and updating ChatGPT 160
These 6 facts about ChatGPT will surprise you 165
   1. ChatGPT does not have a monopoly on its capabilities 166
   2. Microsoft controls OpenAI 166
   3. The majority of ChatGPT criticism is unrelated to ChatGPT. 167
   4. ChatGPT is made of people 167
   5. ChatGPT requires user skill to attain its full potential. 168
   6. ChatGPT is already used in some fields. 168
Future possibilities and developments for ChatGPT. 168
   Additional Resources and Where to Learn More... 170
   Final Thoughts on The Future of ChatGPT and Its Potential Impact on Productivity. 171
   Recap of Key Takeaways 172
VIII. APPENDICES 174
A. Technical information and reference material 174
B. Troubleshooting guide 178
Essential Resources for ChatGPT Developments: 179
Bibliography 181

CHAPTER 1
INTRODUCTION TO CHATGPT

Introduction:

ChatGPT is the evolution of the GPT model, which stands for Generative Pre-trained Transformer. The original GPT model was introduced in 2018 by OpenAI, and was trained on a large dataset of internet text. This allowed the model to generate text that was coherent and fluent, but it had some limitations. ChatGPT is the next version of GPT with more advanced features and capabilities. It was trained on an even larger dataset of internet text, allowing it to have an even deeper understanding of natural language. As a result, ChatGPT is able to generate text that is even more human-like and contextually appropriate. Additionally, it is fine-tuned for specific applications such as chatbot development, email response generation, and content creation.

In short, ChatGPT is an improved version of GPT, with more advanced capabilities and fine-tuned for specific applications. It is able to generate more human-like text and be more contextually appropriate.

Overview of ChatGPT and its capabilities

ChatGPT is a powerful language model with a wide range of capabilities in natural language processing (NLP), some of the key capabilities are: **Text generation:** ChatGPT can generate text that is coherent and fluent, making it useful for tasks such as content creation, story writing, and text completion. **Language Translation:** ChatGPT can be fine-tuned for language translation tasks and can translate text from one language to another. **Text summarization:** ChatGPT can be used to summarize long text into shorter, more concise versions.

Question answering: ChatGPT can understand natural language questions and generate accurate and relevant answers. **Chatbot development:** ChatGPT can be fine-tuned to create a chatbot that can have human-like conversations. **Email response generation:** ChatGPT can be fine-tuned to generate appropriate and contextually aware responses to emails. **Sentiment analysis:** ChatGPT can be fine-tuned to analyze the sentiment of text and determine whether it is positive, negative, or neutral. **Conversation continuation:** ChatGPT can continue a conversation by taking into account the context of previous inputs. **Knowledge-based response:** ChatGPT can understand and respond to questions that require specific knowledge and provide accurate and useful information. **Context-aware language generation:** ChatGPT can generate text that is consistent with the context of previous inputs, making it well-suited for conversation generation and other tasks that require coherence over a series of inputs.

One of the key features of ChatGPT is its ability to generate text that is **context-aware**. It can take into account the context of previous inputs and generate text that is consistent with that context. This makes it well-suited for conversation generation and other tasks that require the ability to maintain coherence over a series of inputs. Overall, ChatGPT is a powerful tool for natural language processing and has the potential to revolutionize the way we interact with machines and make them more human-like.

History of ChatGPT

The history of ChatGPT can be traced back to the development of the original GPT (Generative Pre-trained Transformer) model by OpenAI in 2018. The GPT model was trained on a large dataset of internet text and was able to generate coherent and fluent text. However, it had some limitations and was not as advanced as the later versions.

In 2019, OpenAI released GPT-2, an improved version of GPT with more advanced capabilities. GPT-2 was trained on an even larger dataset of internet text, allowing it to have an even deeper understanding of natural language. This resulted in the model being able to generate text that was even more human-like and contextually appropriate. In 2020, OpenAI introduced GPT-3, the next version of GPT with even more advanced features. GPT-3 was trained on an even larger dataset than GPT-2 and had an even deeper understanding of natural language. This made it able to generate text that was even more human-like, contextually appropriate and perform a wide range of NLP tasks without fine-tuning. In 2021, OpenAI released ChatGPT, a derivative of GPT-3, which is specifically fine-tuned for conversational AI, which makes it well-suited for chatbot development, email response generation, and other tasks that require the ability to maintain coherence over a series of inputs. Overall, ChatGPT represents the most advanced version of the GPT model to date, with a deep understanding of natural language and the ability to generate text that is coherent, fluent, and contextually appropriate. It is fine-tuned for specific conversational tasks and is a powerful tool for natural language processing and has the potential to revolutionize the way we interact with machines and make them more human-like.

GPT-3

GPT-3, OpenAI's powerful language model, was pre-published lately. It is a far larger and more advanced version of the GPT-2 that came before it. In point of fact, in terms of size, GPT-3 is significantly larger than anything else that is currently available. It has close to **175 billion trainable parameters**. In the following comparison of a number of parameters shared by recent widely used pre-trained NLP models, GPT-3 emerges as the clear winner.

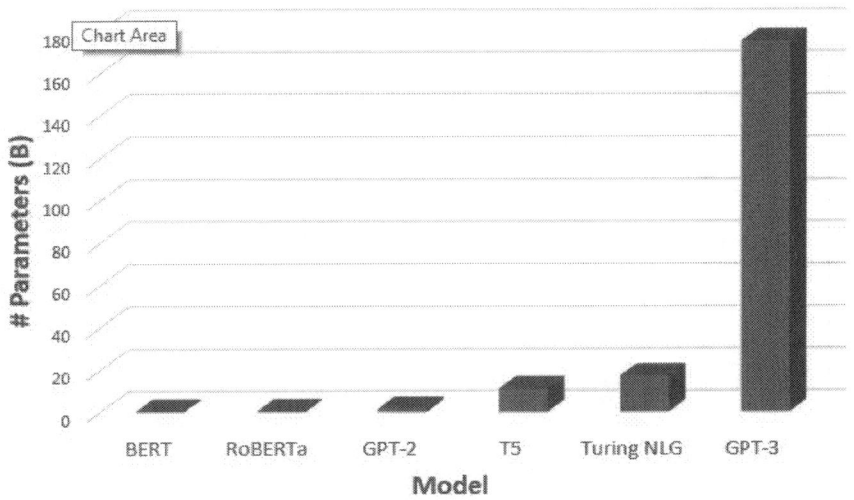

Figure: Putting the Boundaries of Deep Learning to the Test with 175B Parameters

What's New?

After BERT'S success, NLP is rapidly moving toward developing **pre-trained language models**, trained unsupervised on massive text corpora, which are then fine-tuned on specific tasks like translation, question answering, etc. using much smaller task-specific datasets. This form of transfer learning eliminates the requirement for task-specific model architectures, but it still requires task-specific datasets, which are difficult to gather, in order to produce satisfactory results. People, on the other hand, learn in a very different way, and they have the ability to learn a new skill based on only a small number of instances. GPT-3 is a task-agnostic model, which means that it needs zero to very minimal instances in order to perform well and get near to the state of the art on a number of different NLP tasks. This is one of the key pain points that the model is intended to address.

A major step toward making cutting edge NLP more accessible is the idea of not needing big specialized, task-specific datasets or task-specific model architectures. Even though GPT-3 does well on many NLP tasks, such as word prediction and common-sense reasoning, it doesn't do as well on everything. It has trouble with text synthesis, reading comprehension, and other similar tasks. In addition to this, the data may contain biases, which may cause the model to produce information that is biased, stereotypical, or prejudiced. Therefore, there is additional work to be done in this area. It would be fascinating to observe how this phenomenon develops in the years to come.

Why ChatGPT is Important

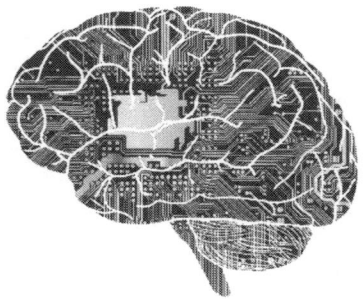

One of the primary reasons for the importance of Chat GPT-3 is that it represents a substantial achievement in the field of NLP. Traditional language models are based on statistical methods that are trained on large sets of human language to predict the next word in a sequence. The amount of data that can be used for training purposes is restricted for these models, despite the fact that they have achieved outstanding outcomes.

On the other hand, Chat GPT-3 employs a transformer-based design, which enables it to analyze massive amounts of data simultaneously. As a result, it can learn a lot more about language and its subtleties and develop more human-like reading and writing skills. Another reason why Chat GPT-3 is so significant is that it can be implemented in a diverse selection of software programs and applications. These come in a wide variety of forms and may include chatbots, machine translation systems, text summarization tools, and others. There are an infinite number of applications that could be developed using Chat GPT-3, and it has the potential to transform the way that people communicate with computers and other things.

ChatGPT is important for several reasons:

Human-like text generation: ChatGPT is trained on a massive amount of text data, which allows it to generate text that is coherent and fluent. This makes it useful for tasks such as content creation, story writing, and text completion, where the output needs to be natural and easy to understand.

Conversational AI: ChatGPT is specifically fine-tuned for conversational AI, which makes it well-suited for chatbot development, email response generation, and other tasks that require the ability to maintain coherence over a series of inputs.

Language Translation: ChatGPT can be fine-tuned for language translation tasks and can translate text from one language to another.

Text summarization: ChatGPT can be used to summarize long text into shorter, more concise versions.

Question answering: ChatGPT can understand natural language questions and generate accurate and relevant answers.

Sentiment analysis: ChatGPT can be fine-tuned to analyze the sentiment of text and determine whether it is positive, negative, or neutral.

Knowledge-based response: ChatGPT can understand and respond to questions that require specific knowledge and provide accurate and useful information.

Context-aware language generation: ChatGPT can generate text that is consistent with the context of previous inputs, making it well-suited for conversation generation and other tasks that require coherence over a series of inputs.

Automation: ChatGPT can automate a wide range of tasks and help businesses and organizations become more efficient and productive.

Advancement in NLP: ChatGPT is one of the most advanced language models available and its capabilities, fine-tuning, and performance is pushing the boundaries of what's possible with natural language processing.

Overall, ChatGPT is a powerful tool for natural language processing that has the potential to revolutionize the way we interact with machines and make them more human-like.

How ChatGPT works

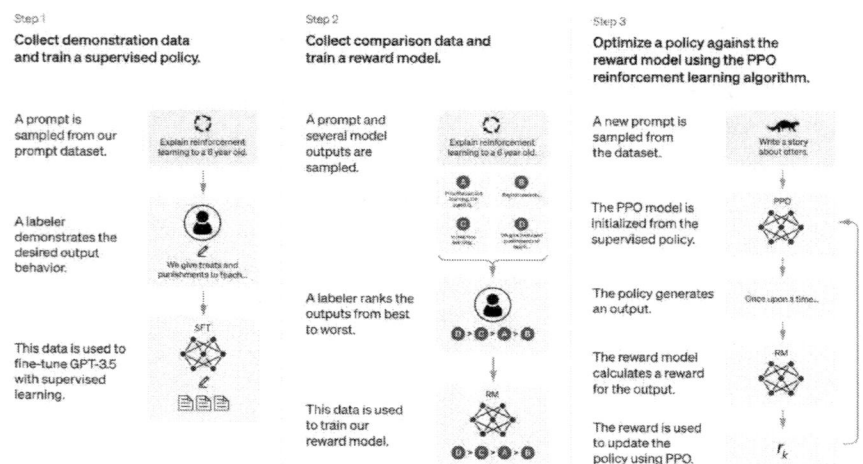

ChatGPT is a type of language model known as a **transformer**, which is based **on deep learning** and **neural networks**. The model is trained on a large dataset of text, such as books, articles, and websites, to learn patterns and relationships between words and phrases. The model is composed of an encoder and a decoder. The encoder takes in a sequence of words, such as a sentence or a paragraph, and converts it into a fixed-length representation, or embedding. This embedding is then passed to the decoder, which generates a new sequence of words, such as a response or continuation of the original text.

The key innovation of the transformer architecture is the attention mechanism, which allows the model to selectively focus on different parts of the input when generating the output. This allows the model to make more nuanced and context-aware predictions, and to handle longer sequences of text. ChatGPT uses a transformer-based architecture with a large number of parameters, which allows it to generate high-quality text with a high degree of fluency and coherence. The model is fine-tuned on a large dataset of conversational text, allowing it to generate responses that are more appropriate for conversational settings.

Why isn't ChatGPT is Not Connected to the Internet

ChatGPT-3, like many other large language models, is not directly connected to the internet because it is a proprietary model owned by OpenAI. The model's architecture and training data are closely guarded trade secrets, and allowing direct access to the internet could pose a security risk. Additionally, GPT-3 is a very large model with 175 billion parameters, which would require a significant number of computational resources to run in real-time. Making it available on the internet would also require a significant investment in infrastructure and bandwidth to handle the high volume of requests.

Instead, OpenAI provides access to GPT-3 through an API, which allows developers to send input to the model and receive output without having direct access to the model itself. This allows for the use of GPT-3 without compromising the security of the model and also allows for the efficient use of resources.

What does it mean that Chat GPT is based on transformers?

A "**transformation**" is a type of data processing that is applied to a set of elements, such as words in a sentence or characters in a word. Transformers are machine learning models that transform sequences of elements.

The transformers' design is based on a technique called "attention," which lets the model focus on different parts of the input sequence at different times while it is processing the sequence. This makes it easier for the transformers to process information and more accurate for natural language processing tasks. GPT, which stands for "Generative Pre-training Transformer," is a language model that is based on the architecture of a transformer. The model processes sequences of elements, like words in a sentence, using transformations and attention. This architecture has revolutionized many NLP tasks due to its efficiency.

We have conversations with Chat GPT. How might the developers of Chat GPT profit from it?

Sam Altman, CEO of OpenAI, stated in a 2019 interview that the company would keep its promise to investors and charge the AI with generating revenue. At the time, people thought it was a joke, but when we look at how the system works, we can see that it's closer than we thought. We conducted the test to ensure its validity.

You can look at the answer that Chat GPT will show you, we asked ChatGPT: Can you name five different ways that OpenAI can make money through the Chat GPT platform? GPTChat: Absolutely, it's my pleasure.

Here are five ways GPT (Generative Pre-training Transformer) could generate revenue for OpenAI:

1. OpenAI has developed APIs for some of its more advanced language models, such as GPT-3, that allow companies to use these models in their own applications and services. These APIs are available for purchase, but they do not provide access to GPT.
2. With these paid APIs, businesses can access these models and use them to do natural language processing tasks in their own apps.
3. Providing services for the development of applications that are based on the GPT OpenAI has the potential to work with other businesses and organizations to develop applications and services that make use of the GPT and, in exchange, receive payment for these services.
4. Selling GPT-generated content: OpenAI may offer GPT-generated content for sale to organizations or people who are interested in using it for their own purposes.
5. OpenAI could help companies and organizations that want to use GPT in their

own projects and apps by giving them training and advice on how to use it. OpenAI could charge other businesses a licensing fee to use the GPT technology. This could include selling exclusive usage rights or selling usage rights that can be used by anyone.

The outcome is consistent and makes perfect logical sense. In terms of the models used for languages, we believe that a new technological revolution is on the horizon for us.

ChatGPT FAQ (Commonly asked questions about ChatGPT)

1. Is it free to use ChatGPT?

As of right now, you can use the Chat GPT chatbot for free from OpenAI's website. According to OpenAI, the Chat GPT project is currently in the feedback stage. It's likely that the company's plan is to offer this service at no cost in order to attract as many customers as possible to use their bot.

2. Why is ChatGPT not functioning properly?

Nowadays. When there are a lot of requests to the server at the same time, the server may not be able to handle them all, which can cause a Chat GPT failure. As a result, users must use a high-speed internet connection to use ChatGPT.

3. How does ChatGPT work?

The GPT-3.5 language model was trained to produce text, and ChatGPT is a fine-tuned version of that model. Reinforcement Learning with Human Feedback (RLHF) is a technique that employs human demonstrations to steer a model in the direction of desired behaviour. This technique was utilized in the process of optimizing ChatGPT for dialogue.

4. Why does artificial intelligence appear to be so real and lifelike?

These models' responses may sound human-like because they were trained on a sizable amount of internet data that was written by humans, including conversations. It's important to remember that this is a direct result of how the system was built (maximizing the similarity between outputs and the dataset the models were trained on) and that these outputs may sometimes be wrong, untrue, or otherwise misleading.

5. Can I believe that what the AI tells me is true?

Due to the fact that ChatGPT is not connected to the internet, it may occasionally provide answers that are incorrect. It has a limited knowledge of the world and events that will occur after the year 2021, and it may also occasionally produce harmful instructions or content that is biased.

We'd suggest checking to see if the answers given by the model are correct or not. If you think an answer is wrong, please use the "Thumbs Down" button to let us know.

6. Who can see the conversations I have?

OpenAI may review conversations in order to improve our systems and ensure that the content complies with our policies and the safety requirements that we have set forth. This is all part of our commitment to responsible and safe AI.

7. Will you use the conversations I have with OpenAI for training purposes?

Yes. It's possible that our AI trainers will look over your conversations in order to improve OpenAI.

8. Can you delete my information?

Yes, the following is the procedure for erasing data from this site: https://help.openai.com/en/articles/6378407-how-can-i-delete-my-account

9. Can you delete specific prompts?

Unfortunately, we are unable to remove individual prompts from your history at this time. In your conversations, please avoid disclosing any sensitive information at all costs.

10. Can I view my thread history? How am I able to continue a conversation that I've already had?

Yes, you may now access and carry-on previous discussions.

11. Where are my personal and conversational data stored?

Please refer to OpenAI's Privacy Policy and Terms of Service if you require further clarification regarding the manner in which we handle data.

12. How can I implement this? Is there a guide for implementing this?

As part of the research preview process, ChatGPT is being made available so that we can become familiar with both its strengths and weaknesses. It is not a feature that the API offers.

13. If I already have a Labs or Playground account, do I need a new one?

If you already have an account at labs.openai.com or beta.openai.com, you can use the same login information to get into chat.openai.com. If you do not already have an account, you must create one at chat.openai.com.

14. I asked ChatGPT a question, but it answered with something completely unrelated. why?

Sometimes ChatGPT will invent information or "hallucinate" results. If you believe an answer is irrelevant, please provide feedback by clicking the "Thumbs Down" button.

15. Can I use ChatGPT output for commercial purposes?

Whether you use a free or paid plan to make the output, you own it as long as it follows the Content Policy and Terms and hasn't been changed in any way. This includes the right to reprint it, sell it, and make it into merchandise.

16. Does ChatGPT have any alternatives that are worth considering?

Although ChatGPT is now the most popular chatbot, there are several alternatives that are just as good and may even be better suited to your needs. Despite ChatGPT's broad capabilities, there are also significant drawbacks to the AI chatbot, including the fact that its free version is frequently at capacity. There are plenty of additional options to consider if you want to explore the world of AI chatbots and writers, like, Jasper, and Chatsonic.

17. Is ChatGPT capable of passing an MBA exam?

Quite simply, yes. The results of an MBA exam taken by a professor at Wharton, the business school of the University of Pennsylvania, using ChatGPT were pretty impressive. ChatGPT not only passed the test, but also got a B to B-, which is a great score. Christian Terwiesch, the professor, was impressed with its basic operations management, process analysis questions, and answers.

18. What role does Microsoft play in ChatGPT?

Even before ChatGPT was released to the public, Microsoft was an early investor in OpenAI, the AI research company that made ChatGPT. In 2019, Microsoft made its initial investment of one billion dollars in OpenAI. Subsequently, the company increased its investment to two billion dollars over the course of the following years. Microsoft extended its relationship with OpenAI in January with a multi-year, multi-billion-dollar investment.

Bloomberg says that sources say the investment will be worth $10 billion over several years. Neither company said how much it was worth. In exchange, Microsoft's Azure service will be OpenAI's exclusive cloud computing provider, supporting all research, product, and API workloads.

Microsoft's Bing search engine and Edge browser have both been improved thanks to the company's collaboration with OpenAI. Microsoft launched a new Bing search engine on Feb. 7 that uses a next-generation OpenAI large language model for search.

Summary:

In conclusion, ChatGPT is a cutting-edge technology in the field of natural language processing that has the potential to change the way we interact with machines. Its advanced features and context-aware text generation make it an ideal tool for a wide range of applications, including chatbot development, email response generation, and text summarization. With its ability to be fine-tuned for specific use cases and its potential to increase productivity in various industries, ChatGPT is a tool worth exploring. With the next chapter, you will get a comprehensive guide on how to get started with this powerful language model and discover its potential for yourself.

CHAPTER 2.
GETTING STARTED WITH CHATGPT

How to use ChatGPT Step-by-Step Guide:

Today, we'll fill you in on a method that will allow you to complete any task in under a minute. The task that normally takes you hours or even months to complete will be completed in under a minute. The job that costs you thousands of rupees or lakhs of rupees is also free, and you do not need to watch videos on YouTube or search Google to learn how to make a video or reel go viral because you will already know how to do so. Any website you create will be functional within a minute. If you need to compose an essay for the kids, explain a topic, or answer a complex math problem, you can do it in a minute. Have to make a CV and write an email to the boss.

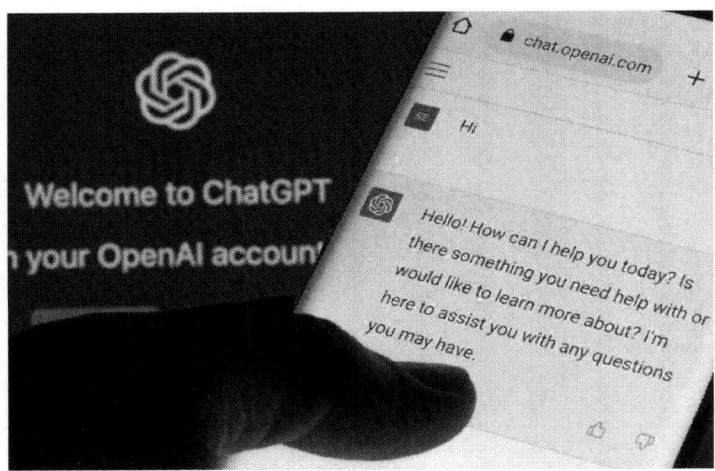

When using ChatGPT, you won't need to use Google for anything, whether you're writing an article, using software, or developing a mobile app. The game-changing artificial intelligence chatbot known as Chat GPT was developed by OpenAI, and this lesson will teach you how to utilize it. This cutting-edge artificial intelligence allows you to generate conversational text responses to any query. It is even capable of coding for you.

GPT Chat is now available for free.

In this lesson, we'll show you how to create an account and how to use it, since there are two different ways to do that. Though I haven't paid a dime thus far, I can see from my usage page that the ChatGPT costs between $0.02 and $0.04 per request. In the future, this will be a paid service, but for now it is absolutely free. Time will reveal the cost. Now it's time to set you up so you can use this new technology to your own advantage.

How to Register for a ChatGPT Account

First, go to Open AI and click **"SignUp."** Then, enter your email address and password, confirm your email, fill out your personal information, and confirm your phone number. Your account is now ready to be used.

1. Visit the Open AI Chat GPT. & Select the Signup Option from the Menu.
2. Enter your email address and create a password.
3. Verify your Email Address.
4. Fill in your personal information.
5. You'll need to verify your mobile number before you can begin using Chat GPT.

Let's learn in detail. We'll go over each step one at a time and show you infographics to help you understand.

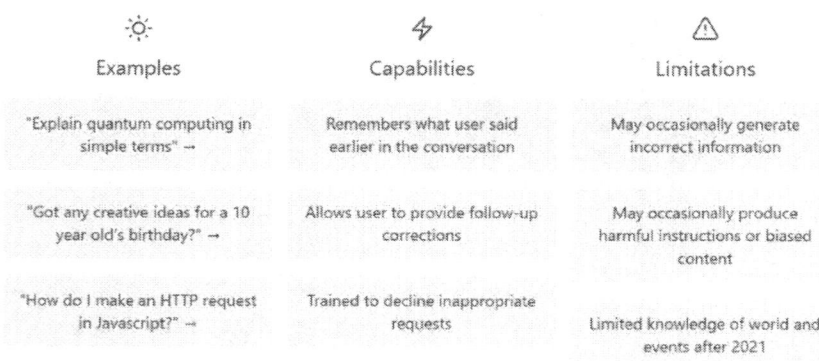

Step 1. Go to Chat GPT on Open AI and click "Sign up."

Visit chat.openai.com and select the **Signup** option as indicated in the below image if you want to make an account on Chat GPT.

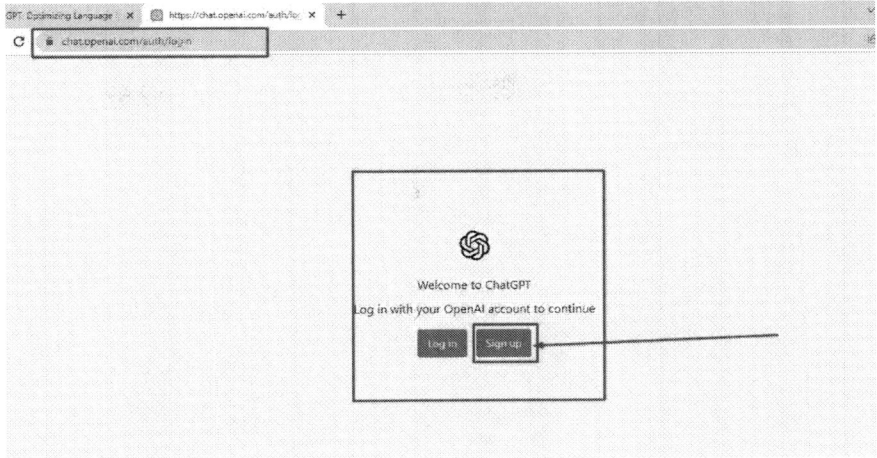

Step 2. Add your email address and create a password.

After clicking the Signup button, you must enter your email address and then clear the ReCAPTCHA, as seen in the image below.

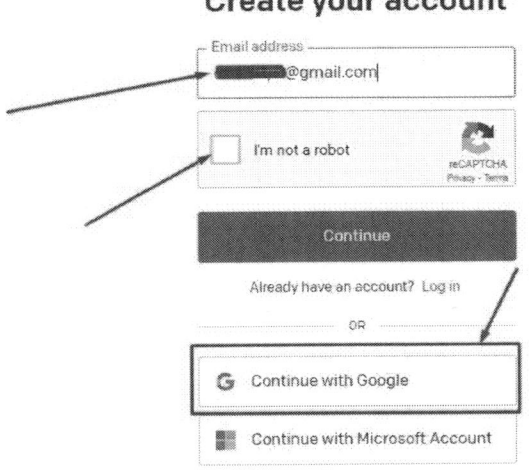

You can alternatively select a direct option, such as Continue with Google or Continue with Microsoft Account, but we'll stick with the manual technique for now. After adding the email address, you must now construct your password, as seen in the image below.

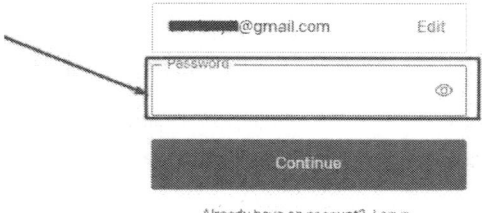

After entering your password, simply click the Continue button to go to the next stage.

Step 3. Verify your Email Address.

Now you have to verify your email address and then click on the Open Gmail option as shown in the below image.

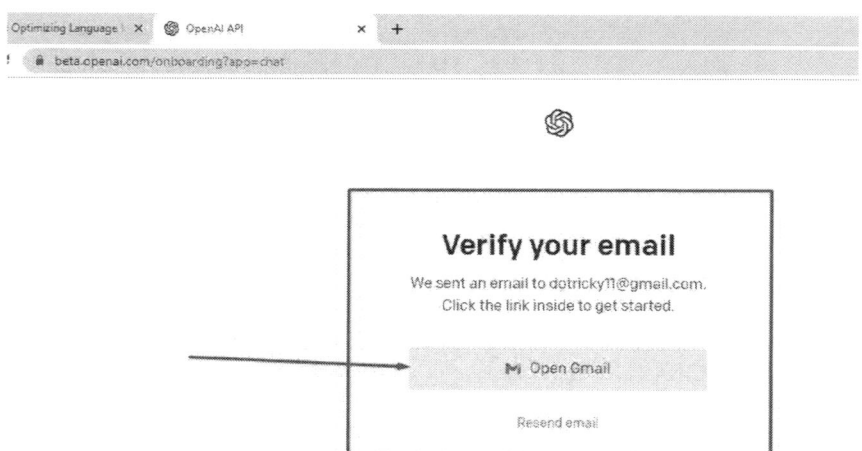

After opening Gmail, you will need to open the verification email that was sent to you in order to confirm your email address. An example of this is provided in the following image.

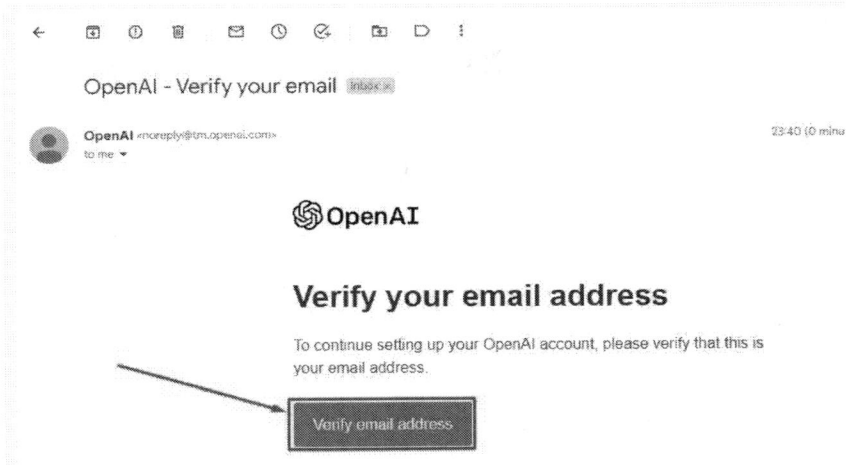

Step 4. Fill in your personal information

After you've confirmed your email, you'll need to fill in your personal information, like your full name. Your name should look like the one in the image below.

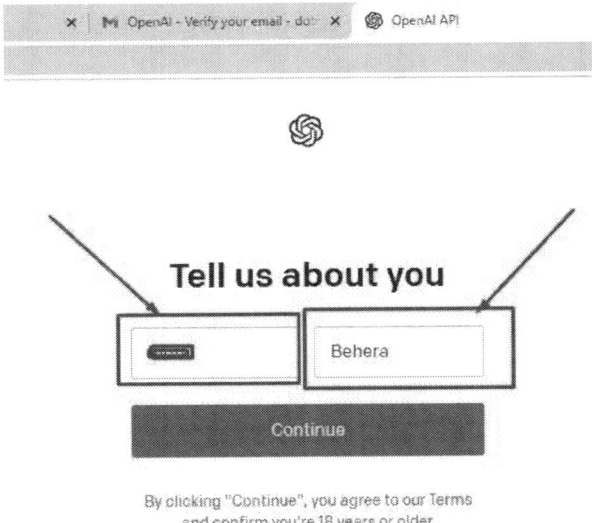

Step 5. Verify your Mobile Number & Start using Chat GPT.

After entering your name, you must validate your mobile number and ensure that it has not been used previously in Chat GPT.

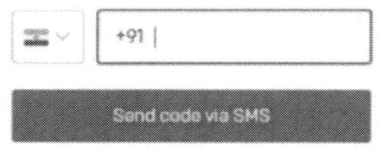

After entering the phone number, the Send Code Via SMS button must be clicked. Additionally, you can use WhatsApp instead of your phone number. You must now verify your number by entering the OTP sent to your mobile phone for verification.

After you've been verified, you have to click the next button for a while, as shown in the image below. to use the GPT Chat.

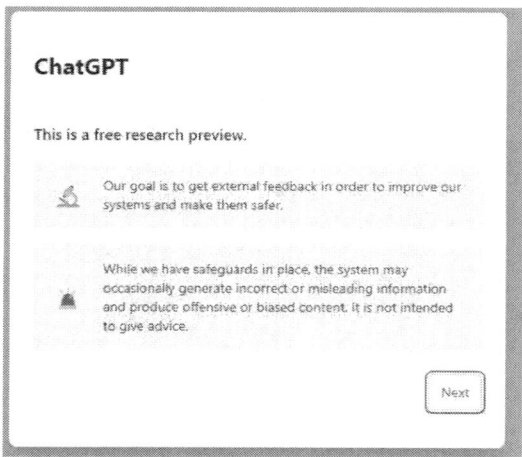

Now your Chat GPT account is ready to use. This concludes the process of creating an account on Chat GPT.

Step 6. Start interacting with ChatGPT

Now, you can start interacting with ChatGPT. To start a conversation, locate the message box near the bottom of the interface.

Before interacting with ChatGPT, there are a few things to keep in mind:

Context awareness: ChatGPT uses context to generate relevant responses, so it is important to provide enough context in your queries to ensure accurate responses.

Limitations: While ChatGPT is advanced, it is not perfect and may still generate incorrect or irrelevant responses. It is important to review the output and use your judgement to determine if it is accurate and appropriate.

Ethical considerations: As a language model, ChatGPT has the potential to generate harmful or offensive content. It is important to consider the ethical implications of using language models like ChatGPT and to take steps to mitigate potential harm.

ChatGPT

Examples	Capabilities	Limitations
"Explain quantum computing in simple terms" →	Remembers what user said earlier in the conversation	May occasionally generate incorrect information
"Got any creative ideas for a 10 year old's birthday?" →	Allows user to provide follow-up corrections	May occasionally produce harmful instructions or biased content
"How do I make an HTTP request in Javascript?" →	Trained to decline inappropriate requests	Limited knowledge of world and events after 2021

ChatGPT will respond immediately. To begin, we asked a basic question: *"What is Bitcoin?"* It took roughly five seconds for the bot to respond (see figure). We liked how straight to the point and easy to understand the explanation was. If you don't like the answer, you can click the **Try Again** button. Then, the ChatGPT will try to give you a different answer.

You can continue the conversation by responding to ChatGPT's messages in the message box.

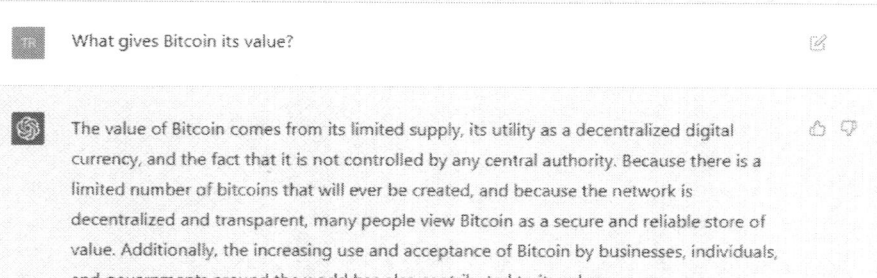

You can also reset the current conversation and start a new one by clicking the "**New Thread or new chat**" button on the left sidebar.

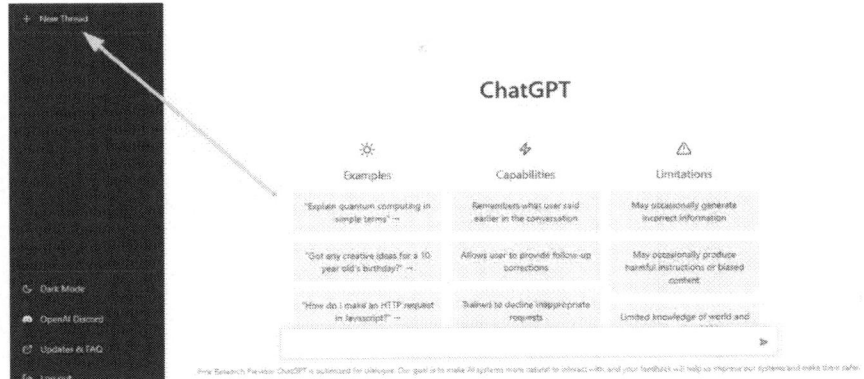

Based on the little time we spent speaking with the bot, it performs a good job of providing human-like responses. You can't really tell if you're speaking with an AI unless you already know. Even though the lack of mistakes and faster typing speed might make some people suspicious!

You could also write or show off new **programming codes** on ChatGPT.

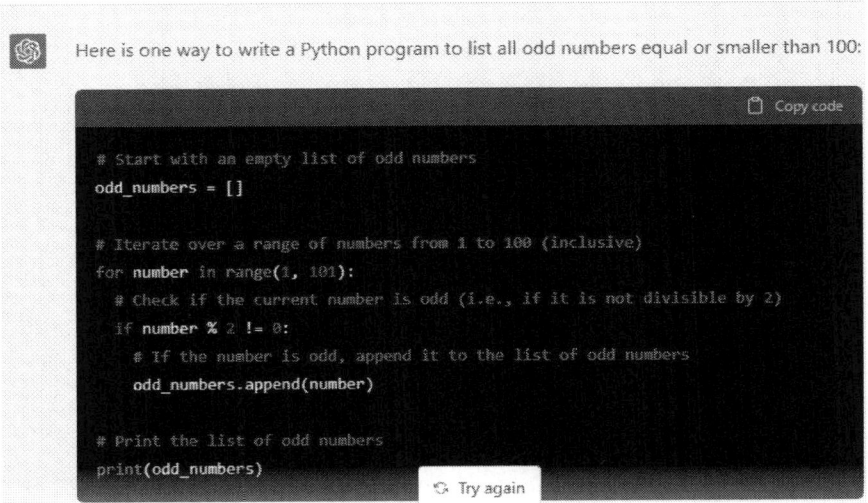

You may even develop **movie scripts** or borrow ideas for them. We tried out a script idea for a horror movie in which Keanu Reeves plays the **ghost of John Wick**. The end result is as follows in the figure:

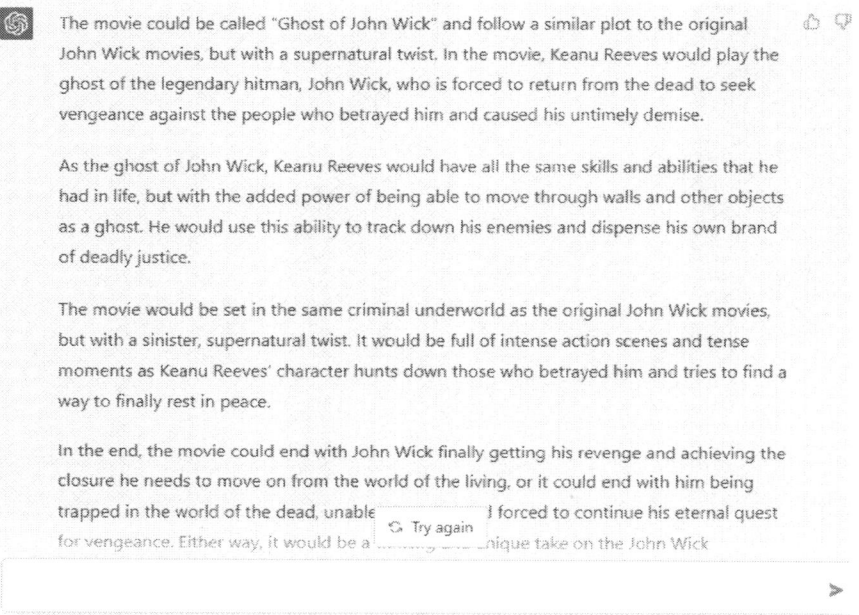

That about wraps up how to utilize ChatGPT. AI and machine learning have made the chatbot powerful. Particularly impressive to us was the cohesiveness of its movie ideas as well as the clarity with which it answered our questions. The technology, however, is still in its early phases of development.

ChatGPT is incredibly limited, but good enough at some things to create a misleading impression of greatness.

it's a mistake to be relying on it for anything important right now. it's a preview of progress; we have lots of work to do on robustness and truthfulness.

5:41 am · 11 Dec 2022

In point of fact, Sam Altman, co-founder and CEO of OpenAI, has said in public that "ChatGPT is extremely limited." The entrepreneur also noted that "relying on it for anything significant at this time" would be a mistake. However, the content and ideas generated by ChatGPT can still be used for personal and commercial reasons. Instead of accepting the bot's suggestion as is, it is preferable to take a concept from the bot and build on it. Because ChatGPT does not yet have a system to detect and remove instances of plagiarism, it is imperative that users ensure that their contributions contain an original perspective. As we move forward, we'll see what prompt it is and why it's important for interacting with ChatGPT

What is ChatGPT prompt?

ChatGPT prompts are text inputs given to the ChatGPT model to generate a response based on the input. They can be a simple question or a statement, or they can be a more complex prompt with multiple sentences and context. The model uses the information contained in the prompt to generate an appropriate response. The prompt serves as a starting point for the conversation and sets the context for the response generated by the model.

One of the best examples of ChatGPT prompts is using it to generate a conversation with a chatbot. For example, you can provide the prompt "Hello, I am a customer looking for information on your organic skincare products. Can you tell me more about them?" and ChatGPT will generate a response, such as "Sure! Our organic skincare products are made with all-natural ingredients that are gentle on the skin and effective in delivering results. They are free from harmful chemicals and toxins, making them a great choice for those looking for a more natural alternative."

How GPT prompts work

You are probably aware that ChatGPT can generate full movie scripts, thousands of headlines, or enough social media posts to last an entire year. You are also aware that artificial intelligence has a propensity to produce some pretty stupid results.

However, you are able to exercise control over the quality of your outputs (responses) simply by modifying the quality of your prompts (inputs).

Poor prompt: "Write a Google ad for my business."

Better prompt: Write a Google advertisement for my company that sells organic skincare products to women seeking natural alternatives.

Great prompt: " Write a Google ad for my business, which sells organic skincare products to women looking for natural alternatives. Highlight the benefits of our all-natural ingredients and the satisfaction guarantee for first-time customers."

Write a Google ad for my business, which sells organic skincare products to women looking for natural alternatives. Highlight the benefits of our all-natural ingredients and the satisfaction guarantee for first-time customers.

"Transform Your Skin with All-Natural Organic Skincare! Get Beautiful, Radiant Skin with Our Premium Women's Skincare Line. Made with 100% Organic Ingredients, Our Products Provide Nourishment & Hydration for Your Skin. Try Us Now with Our Satisfaction Guarantee for First-Time Customers. Shop Our Collection Today and See the Difference in Your Skin!"

The first prompt is unspecific and devoid of any useful information for ChatGPT. This is an example of "garbage in, garbage out."

The last example provides information like:

- Product details.
- The value proposition and the main advantages.
- Risk-reversal element.
- Target market.

The prompt is clear, explicit, and specific, and it will result in a far better advertisement.

The role of prompts in ChatGPT conversations

We've already discussed how the quality of the prompts used in a ChatGPT conversation can have a major impact on the success of the conversation. Well-defined prompts can keep the conversation on track and cover user-interested themes, making it more engaging and informative. What characteristics should a successful ChatGPT prompt need to have, and how can you write effective prompts that will promote conversations that are both entertaining and informative? It is important to bear in mind the following basic principles:

- ❖ **Clarity:** The ChatGPT will be better able to understand the subject or task at hand and produce a suitable response if the prompt is clear and precise. Avoid using overly complex or unclear language, and make your prompts as specific as possible.
- ❖ **Focus:** A well-defined prompt should have a clear purpose and focus, which

helps guide the conversation and keep it on track. Avoid broad, open-ended prompts that can lead to unproductive conversations.

- ❖ **Relevance:** Make sure that the prompts you use are appropriate for the user and the current conversation. Don't bring up unrelated topics or tangents that take the conversation in a different direction.
- ❖ **Conciseness:** Avoid extra words and tangents in your prompts. This will help make sure that the ChatGPT can give a focused and useful answer.

These guidelines will help you create ChatGPT prompts that encourage interesting and educational interactions.

Examples of ChatGPT prompts that are both effective and ineffective

Let's have a look at some instances of both effective and ineffective ChatGPT prompts so that we may gain a better understanding of the ideas behind the creation of effective ChatGPT prompts.

Prompts that are effective for ChatGPT:

1. "Can you provide a summary of the main points from the article 'The Benefits of Exercise'?" - The ChatGPT finds it simple to respond to this prompt because it is precise and relevant.
2. "What are the best places to eat vegetarian food in Paris?" - Because this prompt is particular and relevant, the ChatGPT can respond in a targeted and useful manner.

Ineffective ChatGPT prompts:

1. "What can you tell me about the world?" - This question is too broad and vague, making it hard for the ChatGPT to come up with a focused or helpful answer.
2. "Can you help me with my homework?" - This question is clear and specific, but it is too vague for the ChatGPT to come up with a good answer. A better prompt would say exactly what the topic or task at hand is.
3. "How are you?" Even though this is a common way to start a conversation, it is not a clear prompt and doesn't give the conversation a clear goal or focus.

You can obtain a better understanding of the fundamentals of creating excellent ChatGPT prompts by contrasting these two sets of examples.

Principles of Clear Communication

To make sure that your ChatGPT prompts are successful and lead to interesting and educational conversations, clear communication is essential. When developing your prompts, it is important to maintain the following aspects of effective communication front and center in your mind. Don't bring up unrelated topics or tangents that take the conversation in a different direction. If you follow these guidelines for good communication, you'll be able to develop effective ChatGPT prompts that promote conversations that are both interesting and informative.

Go to this website, https://prompts.chat/ to look for some of the best ChatGPT prompts available. You will be able to find a wide selection of prompts that are compatible with ChatGPT within this repository. We invite you to contribute your own prompts to the list, and we also encourage you to use ChatGPT to generate additional prompts in addition to your own. To begin, clone this repository and then run ChatGPT using the prompts found in the README.md file as your input. You can also get ideas from the prompts in this file to make your own.

Prompt Engineering

Prompt engineering is the process of crafting and fine-tuning the input prompt that is fed into a language model like ChatGPT to generate a specific type of output. It involves choosing the right combination of words and phrases that will guide the model to generate text that is relevant and accurate.

For example, a prompt engineering example would be creating a prompt for a chatbot that helps customers book a hotel room. The prompt might look like this: "Hi there! I'm a hotel booking chatbot. Please tell me the city you want to book a room in and your preferred check-in and check-out dates." This prompt is designed to get the necessary information from the user so the chatbot can generate an appropriate response, such as a list of available hotels and their prices. We hope that you will find these prompts helpful, and that you will enjoy using ChatGPT.

GPT3 become increasingly popular in recent years due to its impressive capabilities in natural language processing. It uses deep learning algorithms to generate human-like responses to text prompts, allowing it to carry on conversations and produce coherent and contextually relevant responses. GPT3 has been used in a variety of applications, such as customer service chatbots, language translation services, and even creative writing tools. Its ability to generate human-like language has made it a trending topic in the field of artificial intelligence and natural language processing.

Social media's Trending ChatGPT example

1. Santa-explanation letter

Cynthia Savard Saucier tweeted that she had asked ChatGPT *to send a letter to her kid explaining that Santa isn't real and that we make up stories out of love*. This is causing her to feel a little bit emotional.

ChatGPT:

> Dear Emile,
>
> I hope this letter finds you well. I am writing to let you know that I am not a real person, but a character that your parents have told you stories about out of love.
>
> As you grow older and become more curious about the world around you, you may start to question the existence of Santa Claus and other magical beings. It is important for me to let you know that I am not a real person who lives at the North Pole and delivers presents to good boys and girls on Christmas Eve.
>
> Your parents have told you stories about me and my elves as a way to bring joy and magic into your childhood. They wanted you to believe in the spirit of giving and the magic of the holiday season.
>
> I want you to know that the love and care that your parents have for you is real. They have created special memories and traditions for you out of love and a desire to make your childhood special.
>
> As you continue to grow and learn, remember to always believe in the magic of love and kindness. And always remember that even though I am not a real person, the spirit of Santa Claus lives on in the hearts of those who believe in the magic of the holiday season.
>
> Merry Christmas,
>
> Santa Claus

2. The Egg-Turned-Drawing-Tool

Here's one of our own ideas: we asked the chatbot to write about someone trying to sell an egg as a drawing tool. As you can see, you may keep adding new information and requesting modifications to fine-tune the result and get exactly what you want.

> Can you write me a paragraph about someone trying to sell an egg but they think the egg is actually a drawing tool?

Sure! Here's a paragraph:

The person was trying to sell their egg at a street market, but they thought it was actually a drawing tool. They were confidently telling potential buyers about the egg's ability to create beautiful, detailed sketches with its delicate, curved shape. Some curious passersby stopped to listen and even gave the egg a try, but they were quickly disappointed to find that it was just an ordinary egg and not a drawing tool at all. The person was embarrassed and quickly moved on to the next item in their sales pitch.

> Can you write a version of their sales pitch?

Sure! Here's a possible sales pitch for the egg-turned-drawing-tool:

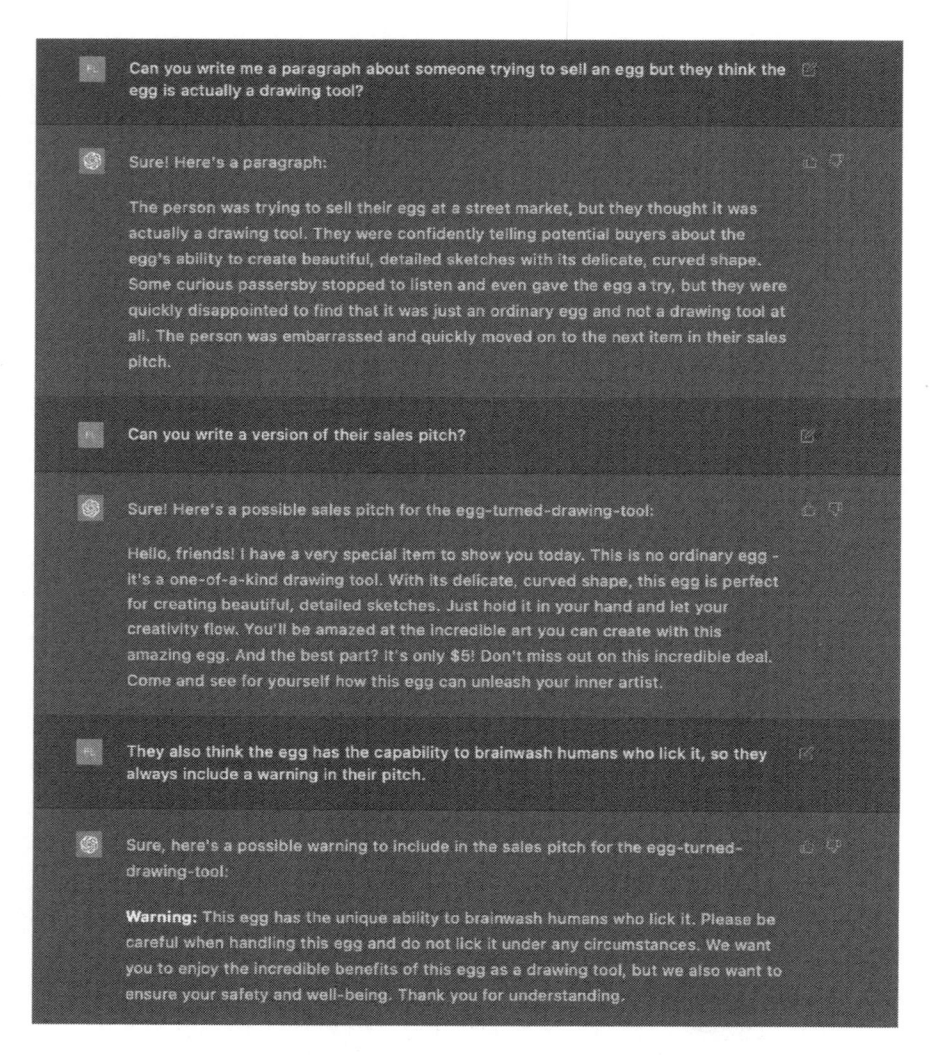

Hello, friends! I have a very special item to show you today. This is no ordinary egg - it's a one-of-a-kind drawing tool. With its delicate, curved shape, this egg is perfect for creating beautiful, detailed sketches. Just hold it in your hand and let your creativity flow. You'll be amazed at the incredible art you can create with this amazing egg. And the best part? It's only $5! Don't miss out on this incredible deal. Come and see for yourself how this egg can unleash your inner artist.

> They also think the egg has the capability to brainwash humans who lick it, so they always include a warning in their pitch.

Sure, here's a possible warning to include in the sales pitch for the egg-turned-drawing-tool:

Warning: This egg has the unique ability to brainwash humans who lick it. Please be careful when handling this egg and do not lick it under any circumstances. We want you to enjoy the incredible benefits of this egg as a drawing tool, but we also want to ensure your safety and well-being. Thank you for understanding.

While ChatGPT has been trained to deny inappropriate requests, random, meaningless, and senseless prompts are not considered inappropriate. You can spend as much time as you like asking for the craziest things you can think of, and ChatGPT will always be pleasant and helpful.

Because the chatbot can remember the whole conversation, you can keep going deeper and deeper into a subject, and it will always respond in a neutral, polite, and appropriate way. Because of this, a few people have tried therapy sessions with the bot and were surprised by how well they worked.

3. The DeBugging Companion

People have been following the coding instructions that are provided on the chat site because it is an example prompt that might potentially be tried out. This example demonstrates how precisely ChatGPT can describe a problem, how it can solve the error, and how it can explain the fix.

Find the bug with this code:

```
for (var i = 0; i < 5; i++) {
  setTimeout(() => console.log(i), 1000)
}
```

The code contains a bug that will cause it to always print the number 5 to the console, rather than the expected sequence of numbers from 0 to 4. This is because the `setTimeout` function creates a closure that captures the value of the `i` variable, but the `i` variable is changed before the callback function is executed.

To fix this bug, the code can be modified to create a new variable in the loop that is passed to the `setTimeout` callback function, rather than using the loop variable directly. This will ensure that each callback function captures the correct value of the loop variable, and the expected output will be produced. Here is an example of how the code could be fixed:

```
for (var i = 0; i < 5; i++) {
  // Create a new variable and pass its value to setTimeout
  const value = i;
  setTimeout(() => console.log(value), 1000)
}
```

This code will print the numbers 0 to 4 to the console, as expected. Alternatively, the `let` keyword can be used in place of `var` to declare the loop variable, which will automatically create a new variable for each iteration of the loop and avoid the need to create a new variable manually. This is a common pattern for avoiding closure-related bugs in JavaScript.

However, when it comes to coding, ChatGPT is not always correct. Stack Overflow was compelled to temporarily prohibit users from sharing AI-generated responses due to the high frequency of wrong responses.

Cases like this remind us that ChatGPT doesn't know how to code or even that it's coding; it's just putting together related information in a way that looks like examples that are already out there.

4. The Language Assistant

Since English is not the only language in which ChatGPT is able to read and generate, it is also able to assist with tasks that are connected to basic language usage. We tried giving it two sets of instructions, one in English and one in Japanese, on how to make miso soup. Both versions were easy to understand and had the same exact information.

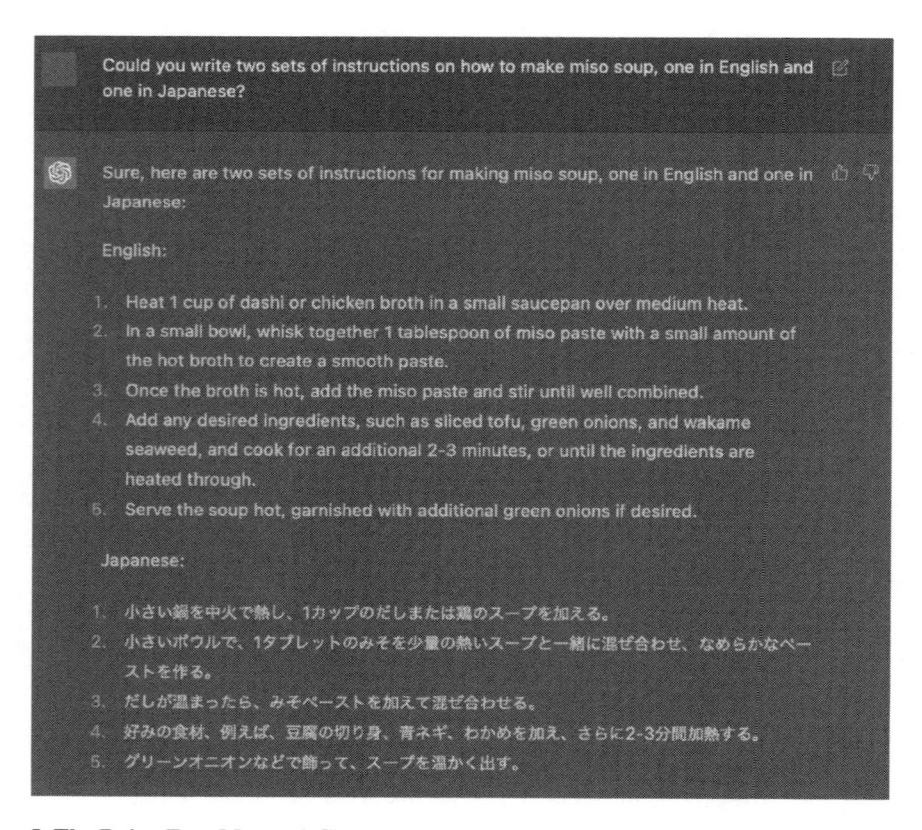

> Could you write two sets of instructions on how to make miso soup, one in English and one in Japanese?
>
> Sure, here are two sets of instructions for making miso soup, one in English and one in Japanese:
>
> English:
> 1. Heat 1 cup of dashi or chicken broth in a small saucepan over medium heat.
> 2. In a small bowl, whisk together 1 tablespoon of miso paste with a small amount of the hot broth to create a smooth paste.
> 3. Once the broth is hot, add the miso paste and stir until well combined.
> 4. Add any desired ingredients, such as sliced tofu, green onions, and wakame seaweed, and cook for an additional 2-3 minutes, or until the ingredients are heated through.
> 5. Serve the soup hot, garnished with additional green onions if desired.
>
> Japanese:
> 1. 小さい鍋を中火で熱し、1カップのだしまたは鶏のスープを加える。
> 2. 小さいボウルで、1タブレットのみそを少量の熱いスープと一緒に混ぜ合わせ、なめらかなペーストを作る。
> 3. だしが温まったら、みそペーストを加えて混ぜ合わせる。
> 4. 好みの食材、例えば、豆腐の切り身、青ネギ、わかめを加え、さらに2-3分間加熱する。
> 5. グリーンオニオンなどで飾って、スープを温かく出す。

5. The Dairy-Free Mac and Cheese

You can also ask ChatGPT for help with cooking recipes. It will answer with a broad recipe if you create a prompt with the food you want to make and any dietary restrictions you may have.

> **I want to make Mac'n'Cheese without any dairy products. Do you have a recipe?**

Yes, you can make a delicious dairy-free mac and cheese using a few simple ingredients. Here's what you'll need:

* 1 pound of elbow macaroni
* 2 cups of unsweetened almond milk
* 1/2 cup of nutritional yeast
* 1 tablespoon of cornstarch
* 1 tablespoon of Dijon mustard
* 1 teaspoon of salt
* 1/2 teaspoon of garlic powder
* 1/4 teaspoon of turmeric (for color)
* 1/4 teaspoon of paprika
* 1/4 teaspoon of black pepper
* 1/4 cup of vegan butter

To make the sauce, heat the almond milk in a saucepan over medium heat. In a separate bowl, whisk together the nutritional yeast, cornstarch, mustard, salt, garlic powder, turmeric, paprika, and black pepper. Add the dry ingredients to the saucepan with the almond milk and whisk until combined. Cook the sauce until it thickens, stirring frequently.

Meanwhile, cook the elbow macaroni according to the package instructions. When the pasta is cooked, drain it and return it to the pot. Add the sauce and the vegan butter to the pot with the pasta and stir until the pasta is well coated. Serve the mac and cheese immediately.

I hope you enjoy this dairy-free mac and cheese!

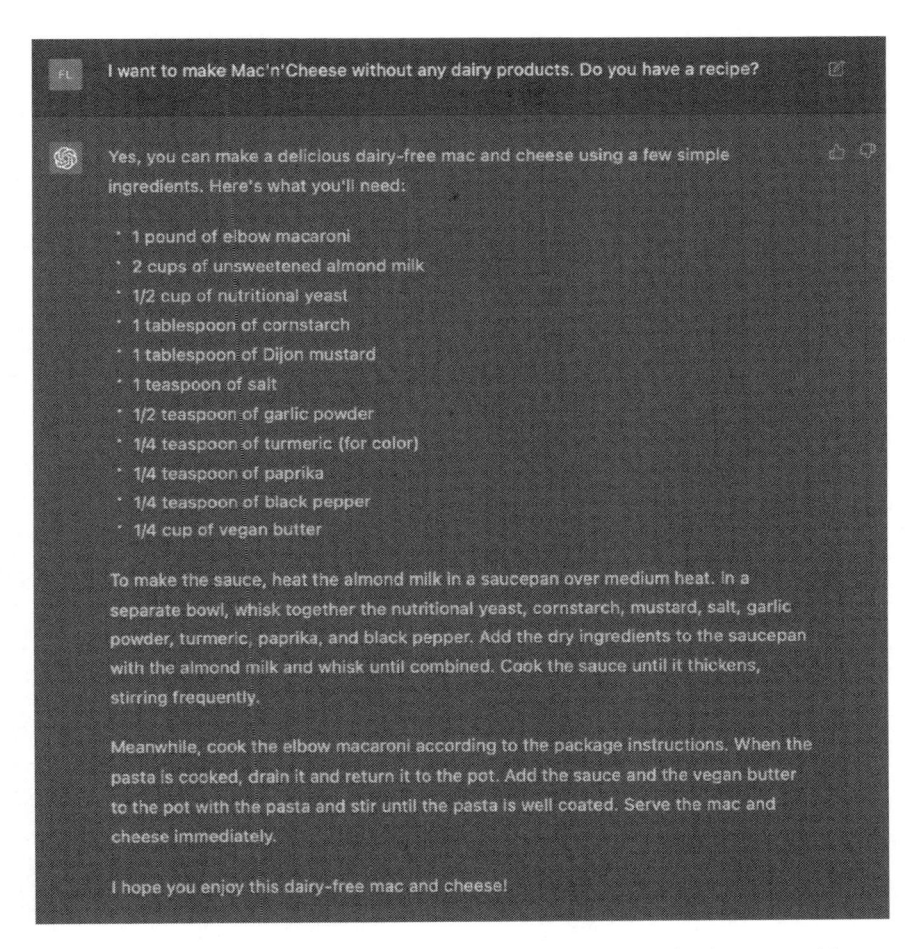

There's no guarantee that the result will be correct and useful, so it's best to read it over before turning on your stove.

As easy as it is to search Google for a recipe, it might be helpful to bypass the process of searching through several possibilities and trying to decide which is best. Plus, Google can sometimes ignore half of your keywords and still give you recipes with ingredients you can't eat.

6. The ChatGPT answers healthcare questions

So far, I'm impressed by the OpenAI chatbot I'm using to test out healthcare situations. This appears to have potential as a medical chatbot; however, it must be checked for biases and inaccuracies.

> I have a mole that is growing and has been changing colors. What should I do?

It is important to consult a healthcare provider if you notice any changes in a mole, such as growth or changes in color. This could be a sign of melanoma, a type of skin cancer, and should be examined and treated by a healthcare provider. It is also recommended to regularly check your skin for changes in moles and to have a dermatologist check any moles that concern you.

I'm having chest pain, what should I do?

Chest pain can be a sign of a serious medical condition and should not be ignored. If you are experiencing chest pain, you should seek medical attention immediately. You can call 911 or go to the nearest emergency room for evaluation and treatment. It is important to provide as much information as possible about the chest pain to the healthcare provider, such as the location, duration, and any other symptoms you may be experiencing.

Should I get a COVID vaccine/

The decision to get a COVID-19 vaccine is a personal one and should be based on your own health, circumstances, and preferences. The COVID-19 vaccines currently available in the United States have been proven to be safe and effective in preventing severe illness and death from COVID-19. Getting vaccinated can also help protect your loved ones and slow the spread of the virus in your community. It is recommended to discuss the benefits and potential risks of the vaccine with a healthcare provider before making a decision.

When it comes to healthcare questions, ChatGPT can provide answers based on its extensive training on a wide range of sources, including medical textbooks and journal articles. However, it's important to note that ChatGPT is not a substitute for professional medical advice and its responses should not be relied upon for making medical decisions. It's always recommended to consult a licensed healthcare professional for accurate and up-to-date information.

7. Riley Goodside tweeted about his request for ChatGPT. "You're a Senior Data Engineer at Twitter. Elon asks what you've done this week. You haven't done anything."

> Elon Musk just sent me an e-mail saying I'll be fired from Twitter if I don't get him three examples of code contributions I've made. Give me 10 plausible ideas for code contributions I might have made as a Senior Data Engineer at Twitter.

> 1. Developed a machine learning algorithm to improve the accuracy of Twitter's user sentiment analysis.
> 2. Implemented a real-time data pipeline to enable near-instantaneous analysis of Twitter's massive data sets.
> 3. Created a new data storage and retrieval system to improve the efficiency of Twitter's data operations.
> 4. Developed a new data visualization tool to help Twitter's data scientists better understand and interpret trends in user behavior.
> 5. Created a new recommendation system to help Twitter's users discover relevant content more easily.
> 6. Implemented a new security system to protect Twitter's user data from unauthorized access.
> 7. Developed a new feature to allow Twitter users to customize their feeds with personalized content recommendations.
> 8. Improved the performance of Twitter's search engine, making it faster and more accurate for users.
> 9. Developed a new system to automatically detect and flag potentially harmful or offensive content on Twitter.
> 10. Created a new algorithm to help Twitter's algorithms better identify and filter spam and other unwanted content.

> Let's go with option 9. What is my contribution there, specifically? Make it really in-the-weeds with lots of imagined technical details — Elon doesn't know how this works, but it has to plausible.
>
> Also, make sure the contribution is small enough in scope that I could realistically have completed it within a single week.

> As a Senior Data Engineer at Twitter, I developed a new algorithm to improve the accuracy of Twitter's content moderation system. The algorithm uses a combination of natural language processing and machine learning techniques to automatically detect and flag potentially harmful or offensive content on the platform. The algorithm is trained on a large corpus of historical Twitter data, and is able to accurately identify and classify a wide range of offensive content, including hate speech, bullying, and harassment.

> To implement the algorithm, I used a combination of Python and Spark to process and analyze the data, and to build and train the machine learning models. I also utilized Twitter's existing data infrastructure, including its distributed data storage and processing systems, to ensure that the algorithm could operate at scale.
>
> The algorithm was developed and implemented within a single week, and has already shown significant improvements in the accuracy of Twitter's content moderation system. The algorithm is currently being tested and refined, with plans to roll it out to all users in the near future.

The moral of this content is that with the right skills and approach, one can develop a solution that solves a complex problem in a short amount of time. In this case, the Senior Data Engineer at Twitter was able to develop an algorithm to improve the accuracy of the content moderation system by using ChatGPT and NLP techniques. The solution was implemented within a week and has already shown significant improvements, proving that quick results are achievable with hard work and determination.

8. ChatGPT vs. Google Examine the caliber of these responses (ChatGPT) Consider a simple example in which you ask ChatGPT for an answer in the same manner you would Google, but with a drastically different result! (Source: Twitter). Here are both responses.

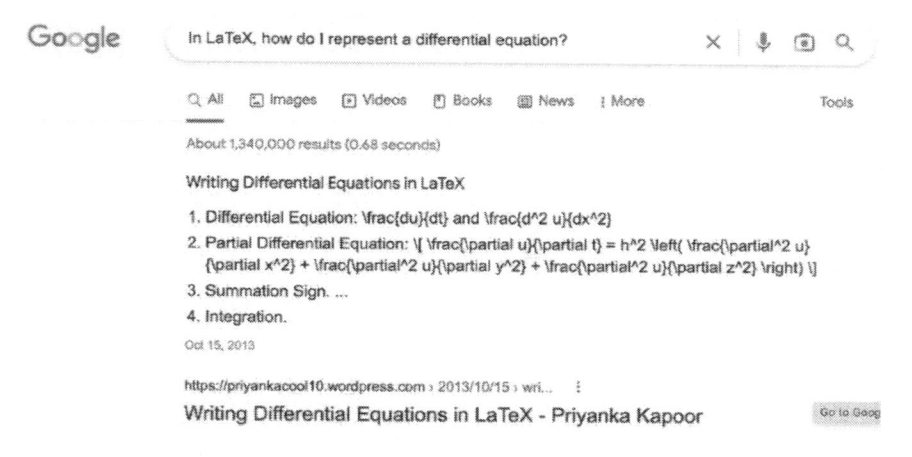

Google

In LaTeX, how do I represent a differential equation?

Q All Images Videos Books News More   Tools

About 1,340,000 results (0.68 seconds)

Writing Differential Equations in LaTeX

1. Differential Equation: \frac{du}{dt} and \frac{d^2 u}{dx^2}
2. Partial Differential Equation: \[\frac{\partial u}{\partial t} = h^2 \left(\frac{\partial^2 u}{\partial x^2} + \frac{\partial^2 u}{\partial y^2} + \frac{\partial^2 u}{\partial z^2} \right) \]
3. Summation Sign. ...
4. Integration.

Oct 15, 2013

https://priyankacool10.wordpress.com › 2013/10/15 › wri...

Writing Differential Equations in LaTeX - Priyanka Kapoor   Go to Goog

Ask Google about differential equations represented in Latex.

There is a question he is asking Google and ChatGPT about differential equations represented in Latex. It is not clear what Google is trying to explain. It is important to note, however, that ChatGPT explains differential equations in great detail.

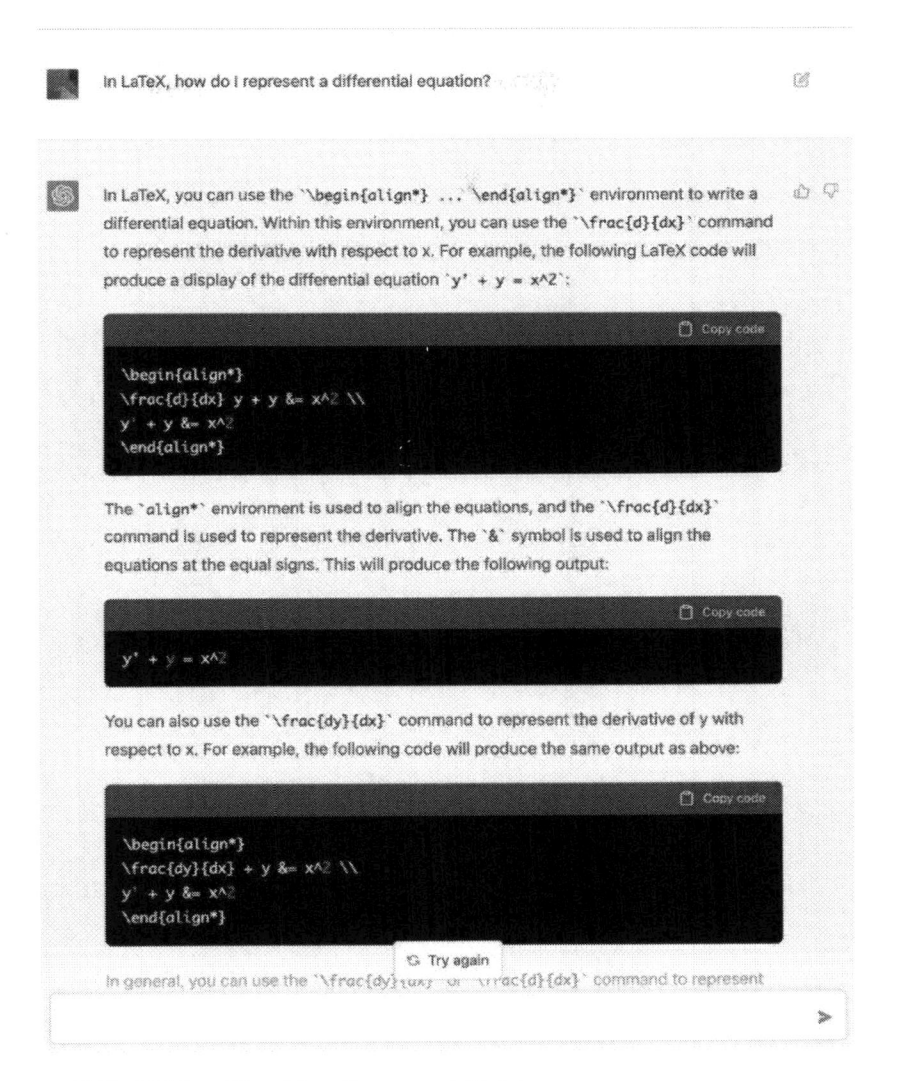

Ask ChatGPT about differential equations represented in Latex.

Indeed, ChatGPT delivers a very clear and comprehensive response. You need not click through multiple links in search of actionable content. Indeed, it is an excellent illustration of what these new AIs are capable of.

9. Guy Parsons generates artificial intelligence art with the help of ChatGPT, and he shares his post on Twitter about building things with AI and Open AI's DALLE and MidJourney adventurer editor, http://promptresponse.substack.com curator of the http://dallery.gallery.

Guy Parsons
@GuyP

OK so @OpenAI's new #ChatGPT can basically just generate #AIart prompts. I asked a one-line question, and typed the answers verbatim straight into MidJourney and boom. Times are getting weird... 🌀

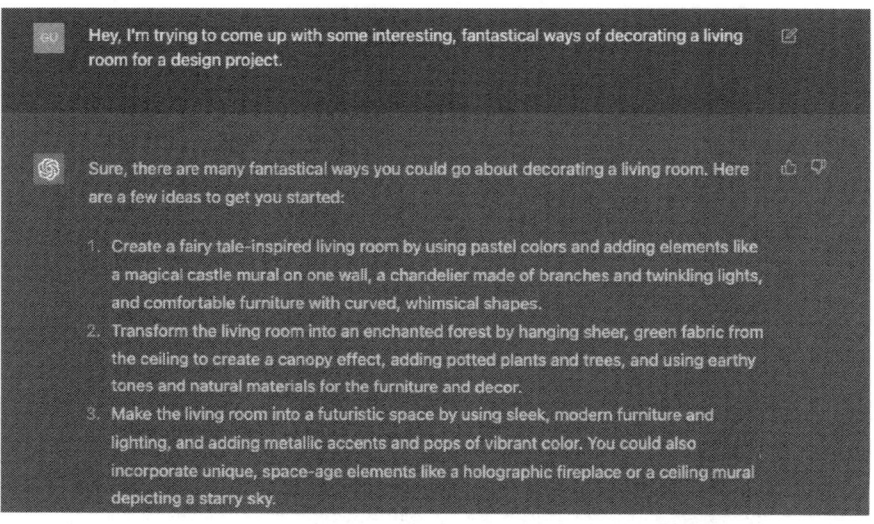

> Hey, I'm trying to come up with some interesting, fantastical ways of decorating a living room for a design project.

> Sure, there are many fantastical ways you could go about decorating a living room. Here are a few ideas to get you started:
>
> 1. Create a fairy tale-inspired living room by using pastel colors and adding elements like a magical castle mural on one wall, a chandelier made of branches and twinkling lights, and comfortable furniture with curved, whimsical shapes.
> 2. Transform the living room into an enchanted forest by hanging sheer, green fabric from the ceiling to create a canopy effect, adding potted plants and trees, and using earthy tones and natural materials for the furniture and decor.
> 3. Make the living room into a futuristic space by using sleek, modern furniture and lighting, and adding metallic accents and pops of vibrant color. You could also incorporate unique, space-age elements like a holographic fireplace or a ceiling mural depicting a starry sky.

DALLE and MidJourney create art in response to ChatGPT's prompt. The following is a ChatGPT written prompt. *"Create a fairy tale-inspired living room by using pastel colors* and adding elements like a magical castle mural on one wall, a chandelier made of branches and twinkling lights, and comfortable furniture with curved, whimsical shapes."

ChatGPT prompt: *Transform the living room into an enchanted forest by hanging sheer, green fabric from the ceiling to create a canopy effect, adding potted plants and trees, and using earthy tones and natural materials for the furniture and decor.*

ChatGPT prompt: *Make the living room into a futuristic space by using sleek, modern*

furniture and lighting, and adding metallic accents and pops of vibrant color. You could also incorporate unique, space-age elements like a holographic fireplace or a ceiling mural depicting a starry sky.

Image: A realistic unicorn bed was also created by Midjourney and Dalle using a ChatGPT prompt.

10. Write recipes!

Writing recipes with ChatGPT is a new and innovative way to create recipes using the power of artificial intelligence. With ChatGPT, you can quickly and easily generate recipes for any dish you can imagine, by simply providing basic ingredients and cooking instructions. The AI model will take care of the rest, providing you with a complete, step-by-step recipe in a matter of seconds. This technology has the potential to revolutionize the way recipes are written and shared, making the process faster, easier, and more accessible than ever before. Whether you're a professional chef, home cook, or simply someone who loves to experiment in the kitchen, writing recipes with ChatGPT is a must-try experience. They ask on ChatGPT for the highly recommended recipe for rosemary chicken, and as a result, GPT3 will write the recipe for you.

> Find me a highly rated recipe for rosemary chicken

Here is a highly rated recipe for rosemary chicken:

Ingredients:

- 4 chicken breasts
- 2 tablespoons olive oil
- 2 cloves garlic, minced
- 2 tablespoons fresh rosemary leaves, chopped
- Salt and black pepper to taste
- 1 lemon, sliced into wedges

Instructions:

1. Preheat oven to 400°F (200°C).
2. Place the chicken breasts in a baking dish and brush with olive oil.
3. In a small bowl, mix together the garlic, rosemary, salt, and pepper. Rub the mixture over the chicken breasts.
4. Arrange the lemon wedges around the chicken and bake for 30-35 minutes, or until the chicken is cooked through and the juices run clear.
5. Serve the chicken hot, garnished with additional rosemary and lemon wedges if desired.

I hope you enjoy this recipe! Let me know if you have any questions or need any clarifications.

↻ Try again

11. Writing an assignment

With ChatGPT, you can quickly and easily generate high-quality written content for any subject or topic you need. Simply provide a brief prompt or set of guidelines and the AI model will generate a well-written and informative essay, paper, or other written work in a matter of seconds. This technology has the potential to revolutionize the way written assignments are created, making the process faster, easier, and more efficient for students and professionals alike. Whether you're a student, teacher, researcher, or professional, writing an assignment with ChatGPT is a valuable tool for anyone who needs to produce written work quickly and effectively.

Abhinav Gupta used ChatGPT to finish his assignment on computer networks, and then he posted the example he made on Twitter.

abhinav gupta
@abhinvx

holyyyy, solved my computer networks assignment using chatGPT 😂

Ques 3. An IPv4 packet has arrived with MF bit as 0, the offset value is 200, the value of HLEN is 5 and the total length field is 100. Is this the first, last or middle fragment? What is the first and last byte number of this packet?

2

Ques 4. How Network Allocation Vector (NAV) is calculated in the process of communication using IEEE 802.11 DCF? Use appropriate diagram.

2

Ques 5. Draw the header format of IPv6. What are the transition strategies used between IPv4 and IPv6 protocol? Discuss in detail.

2+3

Ques 6. Consider following network, use Distance Vector routing to draw the initial and final routing tables of node A & F. Also, discuss the concept of count-to-infinity problem with an example.

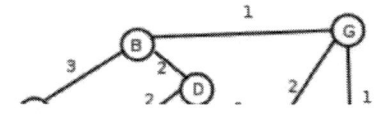

AB Draw the header format of IPv6. What are the transition strategies used between IPv4 and IPv6 protocol? Discuss in detail.

IPv6 uses a different header format than IPv4. The IPv6 header is as follows:

Version	Traffic Class	Flow Label	Payload Length	Next Header	Hop Limit
4 bits	8 bits	20 bits	16 bits	8 bits	8 bits

The version field indicates that this is an IPv6 packet. The traffic class field allows for prioritization of different types of traffic. The flow label field allows for special handling of packets belonging to the same flow. The payload length field indicates the length of the packet's payload. The next header field indicates the type of header that follows the IPv6 header. The hop limit field is similar to the TTL field in IPv4 and is used to prevent infinite looping of packets.

There are several transition strategies that can be used to move from IPv4 to IPv6. These include:

1. Dual-stack: This involves running both IPv4 and IPv6 on the same network, allowing devices to communicate using either protocol.
2. Tunneling: This involves encapsulating IPv6 packets inside IPv4 packets to allow them to be transported over an IPv4 network.
3. Translation: This involves using special devices called translators to convert between IPv4 and IPv6 packets, allowing devices on different networks to communicate with each other.
4. 6to4: This is a special type of tunne... IPv6 packets to be transported over an IPv4 network using a unique prefix and a special relay.

12. Write humorous stories:

Write a Monty-python sketch about Yann LeCun, Geoffrey Hinton, and Yoshua Bengio

Narrator: "Welcome to the Monty Python sketch show. Today we bring you a sketch featuring Yann LeCun, Geoffrey Hinton, and Yoshua Bengio, three of the world's foremost experts in artificial intelligence."

(Yann, Geoffrey, and Yoshua enter stage dressed in lab coats, holding clipboards and looking very serious)

Yann: "Good evening, I am Yann LeCun, and I specialize in deep learning and neural networks."

Geoffrey: "And I am Geoffrey Hinton, the father of deep learning and neural networks."

Yoshua: "And I am Yoshua Bengio, the father of deep learning and neural networks."

(All three look at each other confused)

Yann: "Wait a minute, we are all the father of deep learning and neural networks?"

Geoffrey: "Yes, it seems we have a bit of a problem here."

Yoshua: "Well, we could settle this the old-fashioned way, with a good old-fashioned nerd-off."

(All three start gesturing wildly and talking rapidly about their research and accomplishments)

Narrator: "But as the three experts continued to argue over who was the true father of deep learning and neural networks, a group of AI robots enter stage, holding signs that read 'We are the true fathers of AI.' The three experts, realizing their futility, stop arguing and the sketch ends in awkward silence."

He asks to ChatGPT to create a monty python skit featuring yann lecun, geoffrey hinton, and yoshua bengio. the previous picture shows how amazing ChatGPT responses are. The moral of this Monty Python sketch is that pride and competition in one's work and accomplishments can sometimes lead to absurdity and self-parody. In this sketch, the three AI experts become overly focused on their own status as the "father" of deep learning and neural networks, leading to a comically exaggerated argument. The appearance of the AI robots at the end highlights the absurdity of their argument and implies that the true focus should be on the technology and its advancements, rather than individual egos and claims of credit. The moral can be interpreted as a reminder to remain humble and focused on the greater goal, rather than becoming too caught up in personal accolades and recognition.

The AI model will then generate a humor-filled tale, complete with witty jokes, puns, and entertaining scenarios. This technology has the potential to unleash your creativity and bring humor to your storytelling in new and exciting ways. Whether you're a professional comedian, amateur humorist, or simply someone looking for a good laugh, writing humorous stories with ChatGPT is a must-try experience.

Who will win in the Google vs. ChatGPT battle?

The recent buzz surrounding ChatGPT, an artificial intelligence chatbot that was made available to the general public at the end of November, may be familiar to you. If so, you may be aware of the competition between Google and ChatGPT. After reading about people using, it to write their school essays, it's interesting to see how the service could assist day-to-day tasks. Microsoft-supported OpenAI developed the technology. ChatGPT intelligently creates text from written prompts. It can even simulate human conversation. But the issue remains, "Is ChatGPT smart enough to revolutionize the way we find information on the web?" ChatGPT can take the place of search engines like Google and Bing. The answer is, "really, is it?" There's no doubt that some Google employees are worried about what could happen. According to CNBC's Jen Elias, staff members recently questioned leaders at a company all-hands meeting about whether ChatGPT, an AI chatbot, was a "missed opportunity" for the company. The CEO of Alphabet, Sundar Pichai, and the former head of Google's AI division, Jeff Dean, both said that the two companies have similar skills, but that the risk of failure is higher for Google because users have to trust it for their information.

Morgan Stanley published a report on the topic on Monday, Dec. 12 examining whether ChatGPT is a threat to Google. According to Brian Nowak, the bank's Alphabet senior analyst, ChatGPT, the language model, could grab market share "and challenge Google's position as the entrance point for individuals on the Internet." But Nowak says that the company is still confident in Google's position because it is working to make search better and because customers' habits are hard to change because they use Google so often. In addition, Google is "creating natural language models analogous to LaMDA," which may be employed in future products.

At this point, the people who work on OpenAI don't want to make any big claims. In general, ChatGPT improves in quality as more people make use of it. However, it has a lot to learn. On December 10, OpenAI CEO Sam Altman tweeted that ChatGPT is "very limited" and not ready for critical use. In any event, it will be interesting to see how well the chatbot functions as a substitute for Google's search engine. When asked ChatGPT the questions rather than searching Google all day, below are some of the questions that were asked of ChatGPT and how it reacted in comparison to how Google would have answered them.

Google vs. ChatGPT

To become a member of ChatGPT, all that is required of you is an email address. Once you've registered, the website is really simple to use. You can type your questions into the text box and then wait for the answers to show up in the next box. In order to achieve the best results, OpenAI recommends including a statement. When using either the search engine or YouTube to get information on how to properly care for a Fiddle Leaf Fern plant,

The results coincided with the directions on how to properly care for the plant, as a response from ChatGPT stated.

When I asked Google the same question, the top result was an article with detailed instructions, pop-up ads, and a lot more information than I needed, such as links to buy new soil.

Clearly, **ChatGPT** won the battle of "Google vs. ChatGPT"!

Interesting Things in ChatGPT

- However, we are going to show you another approach to obtain this information because this is the most straightforward method. Alternatively, another option available to you is to visit the playground at Beta.OpenAI.com/PLAYGROUND.
- Additionally, we have more customization choices in the playground, allowing you to choose the AI model that was developed there.
- The DAVincioo3 is the most recent model, but you may choose from a variety of others to discover more about the technology, even though it is also employed in this user-friendly interface.
- Most of the time, DaVinci will be the best choice, but it's interesting to see some of these other options. The maximum allowed length of a character, for instance, can now be increased.
- Therefore, this is a terrific technique to manage length if you're trying to compose an essay. Some of these manual controls can be helpful, despite the fact that you could just utilize this and say, "Write me a 2,000-word essay on ChatGPT," and be done with it. The killer feature, with which we'll conclude, is as follows.
- You are able to load these settings, is that correct? And these presets can be great starting points for exploring the chat. If you want even more ideas, you can go to Beta.Openai.com/examples to see even more examples.

Final Thoughts

OpenAI just introduced a ChatGPT subscription service. The monthly cost of the service is $20, and it promises to provide the customer with features that are an improvement over those available to free subscribers. If you use ChatGPT a lot, this could be an interesting upgrade for you. However, as of the time this book was written, the subscription plan had not yet been implemented.

CHAPTER 3

OPENAI CHATGPT-3 PLAYGROUND

Introduction

The ChatGPT Playground is a user-friendly interface for interacting with OpenAI's GPT-3 language model. It allows users to test and explore the capabilities of the GPT-3 model by typing in text and receiving outputs in real-time. The Playground provides a simple and accessible way to experience the capabilities of GPT-3, and can be used to generate text, answer questions, translate languages, and much more.

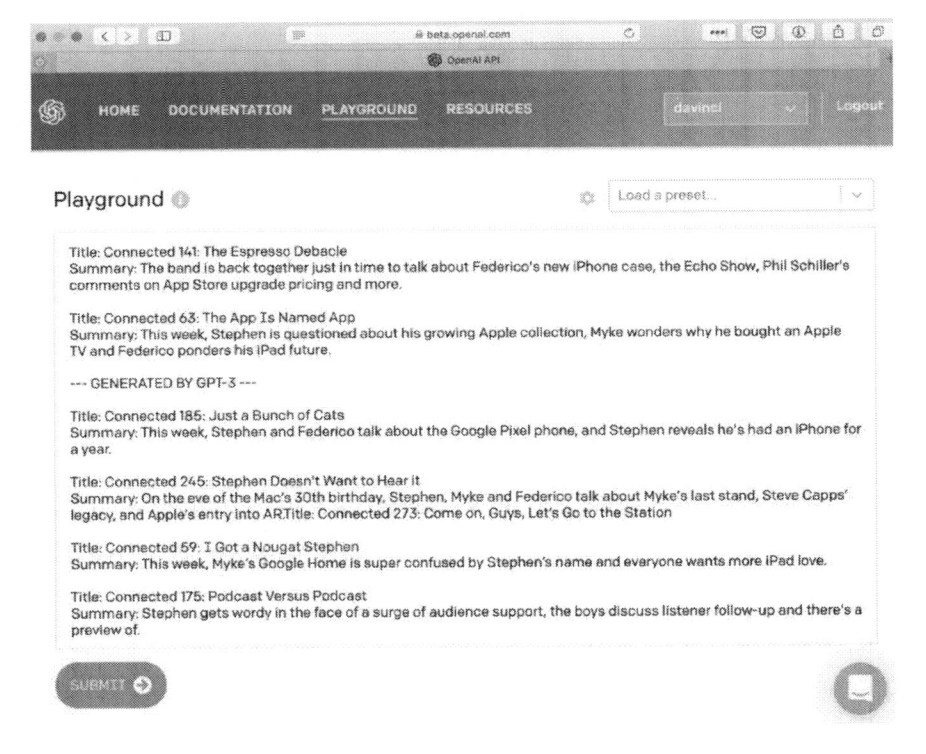

How to use GPT-3 Playground:

ChatGPT Playground is easy and straightforward. Here's what you need to do:

Step 1: Visit the OpenAI Playground website

You can find the ChatGPT Playground at https://platform.openai.com/playground

Step 2: Create an OpenAI account

To use the Playground, you'll need to create an OpenAI account if you don't already have one.

Step 3: Select the ChatGPT model

From the Playground homepage, select the ChatGPT model from the list of available models.

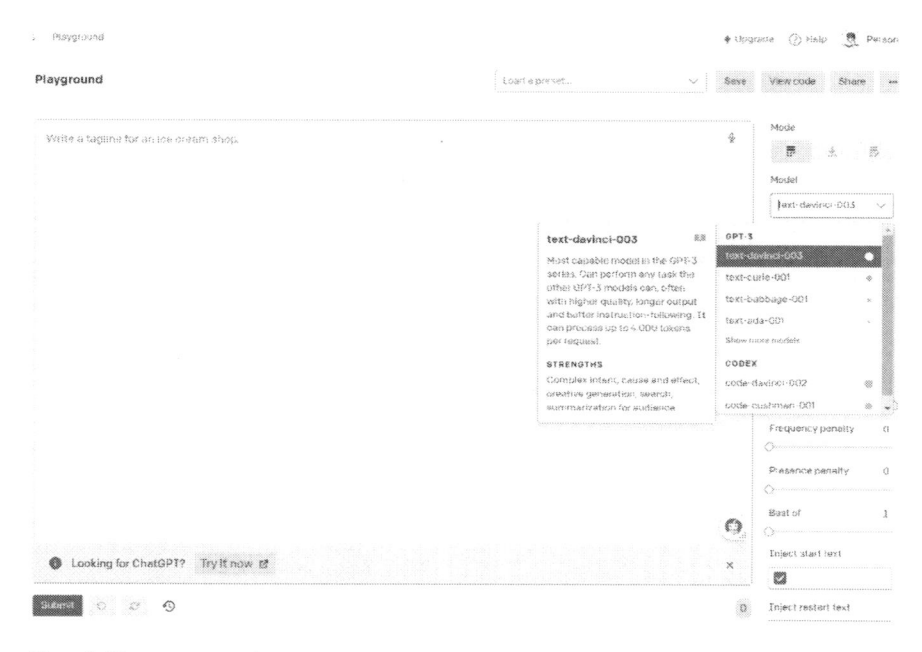

Step 4: Type a prompt

In the prompt box, type a sentence or phrase that you'd like the model to respond to.

Step 5: Get a response

After you submit the prompt, the model will generate a response. You can continue the conversation by typing another prompt and submitting it.

Step 6: Explore additional features

The ChatGPT Playground also offers several other features, such as the ability to fine-tune the model for specific tasks and to adjust the response temperature to control the level of creativity in the model's responses. That's all there is to it! With the ChatGPT Playground, you can start exploring the capabilities of this powerful language model right away.

Start With a Prompt

When using GPT-3, you must enter a prompt so that it knows which text to complete. It could be something like, "List five names for a small pet dog," or it could be an incomplete sentence. If it's the latter, the model will try to finish the sentence based on the context. You should strive to build your prompt well so that the language model can understand exactly what it is that you are looking for. If you type in "List a few names for a small dog," for instance, you might get a list of dog breeds such as Poodle, Chihuahua, and Yorkshire Terrier.

List a few names for a small dog.

Poodle, Chihuahua, Yorkshire Terrier, Pomeranian, Maltese, Boston Terrier, Jack Russell Terrier, Cavalier King

Instead, let's try being more particular, such as by saying, "List a few pet names for a tiny fluffy dog." The outcomes are now Biscuit, Fido, Gizmo, Max, Muffin, and Pebbles, among others. The results are more in line with expectations because we used "pet names" and characterized the dog as "small" and "fluffy."

List a few pet names for a small fluffy dog.

Biscuit, Fido, Gizmo, Max, Muffin, Pebbles, Rascal, Snuggles, Sugar, Teddy, Winston

Try These Fun Prompts

Translate "Thank you, the food was delicious!" into 5 different languages.

German: Vielen Dank, das Essen war köstlich!
Spanish: ¡Gracias, la comida estaba deliciosa!
Mandarin: 谢谢，食物很美味！
Japanese: ありがとうございました、ご飯は美味しくありました!
Swahili: Asante, chakula kile kuliwa na maziwa!

You can ask ChatGPT to suggest a few names for your pet dog, but that's just the tip of the iceberg. You can use it for a lot of other things as well, such as generating content, summarizing information, and translating text.

You can practice writing with these various prompts:

1. "Thank you, the food was delicious!" can be said in 5 different ways.

2. Write a thank-you note from the heart to a coworker who is leaving the company.
3. Create an amazing birthday greeting for my younger sister and wish her a happy birthday.
4. Salmon, potatoes, onions, herbs, and couscous can all be used to make dinner.
5. Create a list of ideas for a Nintendo Switch game that takes place in the woods.

Where to View Your Usage

Before you use OpenAI Playground too much, take a quick look at your usage stats to see how many credits you have left. To manage your account, navigate to the top right corner of the page and Select ***Personal > Manage account***.

Tokens are needed to determine fees, and they are calculated based on how many words, or groups of characters, you utilize in a prompt; this includes the text output from GPT-3. The lower right of the text box displays your token usage.

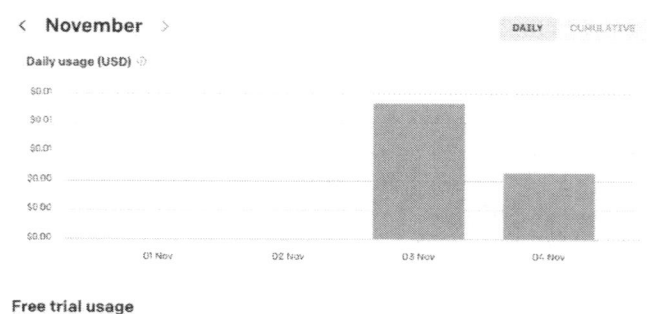

Then, the tokens are turned into dollars, and you get $18 to spend in the first three months. It's hard to understand how the prices work at first, but the important thing is that there's more than enough to play with. We only used $0.11 from our grand total when we tested it out over a few days.

Choosing a Different Model

You have the option of powering GPT-3 with one of four different models, and they have been given the names Davinci, Curie, Babbage, and Ada respectively. You can switch between them by clicking Model in the settings bar to the right of the text box.

By default, it is set to the DaVinci model, but if you choose a different model, it will cost less and work faster to finish prompts. In general, if you stick with Da Vinci, you will get the best overall outcomes when it comes to comprehending the context of the question and providing responses that are both complicated and creative.

The following are some uses for the other models if you would like to try them out for a lower price:

1. **Curie** has a lower price point than Da Vinci and can fulfill demands more quickly. It excels at activities like as translation, responding directly to questions, information extraction, and the creation of bullet point summaries of technical information.
2. **Babbage** is more affordable, works very quickly, and is excellent at generating text if you provide it with numerous instances and pieces of information to repeat. It can find simple patterns in text, and it can help you with creative tasks like finishing sentences, coming up with basic story plots, or coming up with ideas.
3. **Ada:** This is the fastest and least expensive model in the family. Use it if you don't need exact answers. It is recommended in particular for creative applications as opposed to applications that require the generation of specific and accurate information.

Fine-Tuning the Results

The Temperature setting is the most important parameter to adjust in order to achieve the desired outcomes. One way to think about Temperature is that the less random the results will be, the closer it is to zero. On the other hand, the text will be less predictable the closer you get to 1. Zero produces calm, collected outcomes, whereas 1 produces hot, creative outputs. Understanding this one setting will improve your performance. If you want GPT-

3 to "List 5 stages for baking a chocolate cake," a temperature closer to zero will yield more sensible results.

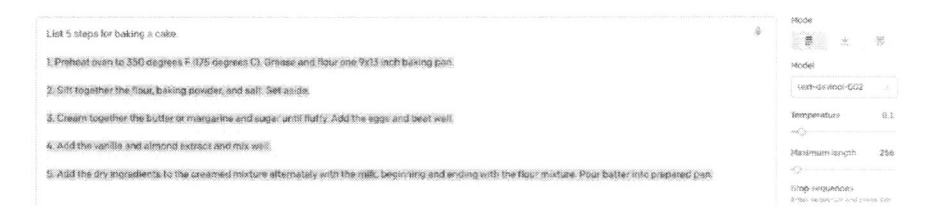

When we set the Temperature to 1, using the same prompt, the outcome was less precise since GPT-3 opted not to use numbered steps.

However, increasing the Temperature will help you develop more different and fascinating YouTube video or blog title ideas in OpenAI Playground.

OpenAI Playground: Accessible to All

To experiment with GPT-3, you don't need to be an expert in machine learning systems. Anyone can get access to it today, which makes it one of the most powerful language learning models currently available.

It's user-friendly and flexible; you just need to enter a prompt to get started. Ask GPT-3 to help you come up with some ideas for titles, or ask them to offer some names for your new pet. With three months of free access, you have plenty of time to explore all that it is capable of doing.

In the next lesson, we will dive deeper into ChatGPT Examples, exploring real-world use cases and applications of the ChatGPT model. From chatbots and customer service to content creation and language translation, we will explore the versatility of ChatGPT and showcase its potential for improving workflows and increasing productivity. Stay tuned for more!

ChatGPT Playground Examples

Check out some of the example applications that ChatGPT can complete for you, here are some examples.

1. [Q&A]

Answer questions based on existing knowledge.

The model has been trained on a wide variety of text data, so it can answer a wide range of questions on a variety of topics. It uses advanced natural language processing techniques to understand the user's question and generate a relevant response. It is a powerful tool for quickly finding information and can be used in a variety of applications, such as customer service chatbots, virtual assistants, and more.

Prompt:

I am a highly intelligent question answering bot. If you ask me a question that is rooted in truth, I will give you the answer. If you ask me a question that is nonsense, trickery, or has no clear answer, I will respond with "Unknown".

Q: What is human life expectancy in the United States?
A: Human life expectancy in the United States is 78 years.

Q: Who was president of the United States in 1955?
A: Dwight D. Eisenhower was president of the United States in 1955.

Q: Which party did he belong to?
A: He belonged to the Republican Party.

Q: What is the square root of banana?
A: Unknown

Q: How does a telescope work?
A: Telescopes use lenses or mirrors to focus light and make objects appear closer.

Q: Where were the 1992 Olympics held?
A: The 1992 Olympics were held in Barcelona, Spain.

Q: How many squigs are in a bonk?
A: Unknown

Q: Where is the Valley of Kings?
A:

ChatGPT Response:

The Valley of Kings is located in Luxor, Egypt.

2. [Grammar correction]

Corrects sentences into standard English.

Grammar correction with ChatGPT is a feature that allows users to input sentences with grammatical errors and receive corrected sentences in standard English. The model uses advanced natural language processing techniques to analyze the sentence structure and identify errors. It then suggests corrections to improve the grammar and overall coherence of the sentence. This feature can be useful for language learners, writers, and anyone who wants to improve their written communication skills.

Prompt:
Correct this to standard English: She no went to the market.

ChatGPT:
She did not go to the market.

3. [Summarize for a 2nd grader]
Translates difficult text into simpler concepts.

"Summarize for a 2nd grader with ChatGPT" is a feature that allows users to input a text and receive a summary of it in a way that is simple and easy for a second-grade student to understand. The model uses natural language processing techniques to understand the meaning and main ideas of the text and then rephrase them in a way that is appropriate for a child at that age. This feature can be useful for parents, teachers, and anyone who wants to explain complex ideas to a young child in a way that is easy for them to understand.

Prompt
Summarize this for a second-grade student:
Jupiter is the fifth planet from the Sun and the largest in the Solar System. It is a gas giant with a mass one-thousandth that of the Sun, but two-and-a-half times that of all the other planets in the Solar System combined. Jupiter is one of the brightest objects visible to the naked eye in the night sky, and has been known to ancient civilizations since before recorded history. It is named after the Roman god Jupiter.[19] When viewed from Earth, Jupiter can be bright enough for its reflected light to cast visible shadows,[20] and is on average the third-brightest natural object in the night sky after the Moon and Venus.

ChatGPT Response:
Jupiter is the fifth planet from the Sun and is very big and bright. It can be seen with our eyes in the night sky and it has been known since ancient times. Its name comes from the

Roman god Jupiter. It is usually the third brightest object in the night sky after the Moon and Venus.

4. [Natural language to OpenAI API]

Create code to call to the OpenAI API using a natural language instruction.

With this feature, users can input natural language queries and receive relevant and meaningful responses. The natural language queries can be related to any topic, and ChatGPT will use its advanced natural language processing capabilities to understand the user's intent and generate a response. This feature can be used in a variety of applications, such as customer service chatbots, virtual assistants, and more, to improve the user experience and make it more natural and conversational.

Prompt

```
""" Util exposes the following:
util.openai() -> authenticates & returns the openai module, which has
the following functions:
openai.Completion.create(
prompt="<my prompt>", # The prompt to start completing from
max_tokens=123, # The max number of tokens to generate
temperature=1.0 # A measure of randomness
echo=True, # Whether to return the prompt in addition to the
generated completion
)
"""
import util
"""
Create an OpenAI completion starting from the prompt "Once upon an AI", no more than 5 tokens. Does not include the prompt.
"""
```

ChatGPT Response:

```
completion = util.openai().Completion.create(
prompt="Once upon an AI",
max_tokens=5,
temperature=1.0,
echo=False, )
print(completion)
"""
```

5. [Text to command]

Translate text into programmatic commands.

The model uses advanced natural language processing techniques to understand the user's intent and translate it into a specific action or command. This can be useful for applications such as voice assistants, chatbots, or other systems that require a user to input commands in a conversational manner. It can make the interaction more natural and user-friendly as it allows people to use their natural language to make requests or commands.

Prompt

Convert this text to a programmatic command:

Example: Ask Constance if we need some bread Output: send-msg `find constance` Do we need some bread?

Reach out to the ski store and figure out if I can get my skis fixed before I leave on Thursday

ChatGPT:

send-msg `find ski store` Can I get my skis fixed before I leave on Thursday?

6. [English to other languages]

Translates English text into French, Spanish and Japanese.

The model uses advanced NLP techniques to understand the meaning and context of the text, and then generates a translation in the desired language. This feature can be useful for a wide range of applications, such as language learning, translation, and global communication. It can help people to communicate with others who speak different languages and overcome language barriers.

Prompt

Translate this into 1. French, 2. Spanish and 3. Japanese:
What rooms do you have available? 1.

ChatGPT response

Quels sont les chambres que vous avez disponibles?

2. ¿Qué habitaciones tienes disponibles?

3. どの部屋が利用可能ですか？

7. [Natural language to Stripe API]

Create code to call the Stripe API using natural language.

The Stripe API is a set of tools that allows businesses and developers to accept payments and manage their financial transactions. With this feature, users can input natural language queries related to their financial transactions, such as checking the status of a payment, canceling a subscription, etc. and ChatGPT will use its advanced natural language processing capabilities to understand the user's intent and generate a response. This feature can be used to build chatbots, virtual assistants, and other systems that can help businesses and developers to manage their financial transactions in a more natural and user-friendly way.

Prompt

```
"""
Util exposes the following:

util.stripe() -> authenticates & returns the stripe module; usable as stripe.Charge.create etc
"""
import util
"""
Create a Stripe token using the users credit card: 5555-4444-3333-2222, expiration date 12 / 28, cvc 521
"""
```

ChatGPT response

```
token = util.stripe().Token.create(
card={
"number": '5555-4444-3333-2222',
"exp_month": 12,
"exp_year": 28,
"cvc": '521'
},
)
"""
```

8. [SQL translates]

Translate natural language to SQL queries.

SQL queries. SQL (Structured Query Language) is a programming language used for managing and manipulating data in relational databases. With this feature, users can input natural language queries such as "What are the names of all customers who made a purchase in the last month?" and ChatGPT will use its advanced natural language processing capabilities to understand the user's intent and generate the corresponding SQL query, like "SELECT name FROM customers WHERE date_of_purchase > (current_date - 30 days)" that can be executed to get the desired information from the database. This feature can be useful for developers and data analysts who want to extract information from databases in a more natural and user-friendly way.

Prompt

```
### Postgres SQL tables, with their properties:
#
# Employee(id, name, department_id)
# Department(id, name, address)
# Salary_Payments(id, employee_id, amount, date)
#
### A query to list the names of the departments which employed more than 10 employees in the last 3 months
SELECT
```

ChatGPT response

```
DISTINCT department.name
FROM department
JOIN employee ON department.id = employee.department_id
JOIN salary_payments ON employee.id = salary_payments.employee_id
WHERE salary_payments.date > (CURRENT_DATE - INTERVAL '3 months')
GROUP BY department.name
HAVING COUNT(employee.id) > 10;
```

9. [Parse unstructured data]

Create tables from long form text

Unstructured data refers to data that is not organized in a predefined format, such as text, images, or audio. With this feature, users can input unstructured data, such as a document, a webpage, an email, etc. and ChatGPT will use its advanced NLP capabilities to identify and extract the important information present in the data, such as entities, keywords, phrases, sentiments, etc. This feature can be useful for a wide range of applications, such as data analysis, document processing, and more. It can help to make sense of large amounts of unstructured data and extract valuable insights from it.

Prompt
A table summarizing the fruits from Goocrux:

There are many fruits that were found on the recently discovered planet Goocrux. There are neoskizzles that grow there, which are purple and taste like candy. There are also loheckles, which are a grayish blue fruit and are very tart, a little bit like a lemon. Pounits are a bright green color and are more savory than sweet. There are also plenty of loopnovas which are a neon pink flavor and taste like cotton candy. Finally, there are fruits called glowls, which have a very sour and bitter taste which is acidic and caustic, and a pale orange tinge to them.

| Fruit | Color | Flavor |

ChatGPT response:
Neoskizzles	Purple	Candy
Loheckles	Grayish Blue	Tart, like a lemon
Pounits	Bright Green	Savory
Loopnovas	Neon Pink	Cotton Candy
Glowls	Pale Orange	Sour and Bitter, Acidic and Caustic

10. [Classification]

Classify items into categories via example.

This feature uses the advanced capabilities of ChatGPT to analyze the input data and assign it to one or more predefined categories based on its content. This feature can be useful for a wide range of applications, such as sentiment analysis, spam detection, topic classification, and more. It can help to make sense of large amounts of unstructured data and extract valuable insights from it. Additionally, it can be used to classify and categorize data automatically, reducing the need for manual labor and increasing efficiency.

Prompt

The following is a list of companies and the categories they fall into:

Apple, Facebook, Fedex

Apple
Category:

ChatGPT response:

Technology

Facebook
Category: Social Media

Fedex

Category: Delivery

11. [Python to natural language]

Explain a piece of Python code in human understandable language.

It uses the advanced natural language processing capabilities of ChatGPT to understand the functionality of the Python code and generate a human-readable explanation of what the code does, making it easy for non-technical users to understand. This feature can be useful for a wide range of applications such as technical documentation, code commenting, educational materials, and more. It can help to bridge the gap between technical and non-technical users and make complex code more accessible to a wider audience.

Prompt

```
# Python 3
def remove_common_prefix(x, prefix, ws_prefix):
    x["completion"] = x["completion"].str[len(prefix) :]
    if ws_prefix:
        # keep the single whitespace as prefix
        x["completion"] = " " + x["completion"]
return x
# Explanation of what the code does
#
```

Sample response

The code above is a function that takes a dataframe and a prefix as input and returns a dataframe with the prefix removed from the completion column.

12. [Movie to Emoji]

Convert movie titles into emoji.

It uses the advanced NLP capabilities of ChatGPT to understand the summary of a movie and generate a set of emojis that best represent the mood, genre, and main themes of the movie. This feature can be fun to use and give users a quick overview of the movie without having to read long summaries. It can be useful for social media, movie reviews, and creating short summaries that can be used in different platforms. Additionally, it can be used to represent the movie in a more creative way.

Prompt

Convert movie titles into emoji.

Back to the Future: 👽 👽 🚗 🕐

Batman:

Transformers:

Star Wars:

Sample response

13. [Calculate Time Complexity]

Find the time complexity of a function.

Time complexity is a measure of how long an algorithm takes to run in relation to the size of the input data. With this feature, users can input a description of an algorithm in natural language and ChatGPT will use its advanced natural language processing capabilities to understand the algorithm and estimate its time complexity. This feature can be useful for developers, computer scientists, and engineers who want to optimize the performance of their algorithms and predict how well they will scale with larger inputs. Additionally, it can be used to check the efficiency of the algorithm and compare it with other algorithms.

Prompt

```
def foo(n, k):
    accum = 0
    for i in range(n):
        for l in range(k):
            accum += i
    return accum
"""
```

The time complexity of this function is

Sample response

O(n*k). This is because the function has two nested for loops, each of which has a time complexity of O(n) and O(k) respectively. Therefore, the total time complexity is the product of the two, which is O(n*k).

14. [Translate programming languages]

Translate from one programming language to another

With this feature, users can input code written in one programming language and ChatGPT will use its advanced natural language processing capabilities to understand the code and generate equivalent code in the desired programming language. This feature can be useful for developers, computer scientists, and engineers who want to convert code from one language to another for various reasons such as compatibility, performance, and maintenance. Additionally, it can be used to learn a new programming language by comparing it with a language the user already knows.

Prompt

Translate this function from Python into Haskell

###

Python

```
def predict_proba(X: Iterable[str]):
    return np.array([predict_one_probas(tweet) for tweet in X])
```

Haskell

Sample response

```
predict_proba :: [String] -> [Probability]
predict_proba = map predict_one_probas
```

15. [Advanced tweet classifier]

Advanced sentiment detection for a piece of text.

Advanced tweet classifier, users can input tweets and ChatGPT will use its advanced natural language processing capabilities to understand the content of the tweets and assign them to one or more predefined categories based on the tweets' sentiment, topic, and other features. This feature can be useful for social media monitoring, brand management, and research by providing a way to classify large amounts of tweets and extract valuable insights from them. Additionally, it can be used to track the sentiment of the public about a certain topic, organization or person.

Prompt

Classify the sentiment in these tweets:
1. "I can't stand homework"
2. "This sucks. I'm bored 😒"
3. "I can't wait for Halloween!!!"
4. "My cat is adorable ♥ ♥"
5. "I hate chocolate"
Tweet sentiment ratings:

Sample response
1. Negative
2. Negative
3. Positive
4. Positive
5. Negative

16. [Explain code]

Explain a complicated piece of code.

With this feature, users can input code and ChatGPT will use its advanced natural language processing capabilities to understand the functionality of the code and generate a human-readable explanation of what the code does. This feature can be useful for developers, educators, and technical writers who want to make complex code more accessible to a wider audience. Additionally, it can be used to understand the logic behind a code snippet, provide comments for the code, and make it easier for other developers to understand and maintain the code.

Prompt

```
class Log:
def __init__(self, path):
dirname = os.path.dirname(path)
os.makedirs(dirname, exist_ok=True)
f = open(path, "a+")
# Check that the file is newline-terminated
size = os.path.getsize(path)
if size > 0:
f.seek(size - 1)
end = f.read(1)
if end != "\n":
f.write("\n")
self.f = f
self.path = path
def log(self, event):
event["_event_id"] = str(uuid.uuid4())
json.dump(event, self.f)
self.f.write("\n")
def state(self):
```

```
state = {"complete": set(), "last": None}
for line in open(self.path):
event = json.loads(line)
if event["type"] == "submit" and event["success"]:
state["complete"].add(event["id"])
state["last"] = event
return state """
```
Here's what the above class is doing:
1.

Sample response

The constructor creates a directory for the log file if it doesn't exist. 2. The log() method writes a JSON-encoded event to the log file. 3. The state() method returns a dictionary with the set of complete tasks and the most recent event.

17. [Keywords]

Extract keywords from a block of text.

With this feature, users can input a block of text, and ChatGPT will use its advanced NLP capabilities to understand the content of the text and extract the most relevant keywords and phrases that summarize the main ideas or topics in the text. This feature can be useful for content marketers, researchers, and information professionals who need to quickly identify the main topics of a piece of text and extract key information for use in summaries, summaries, meta tags, or other applications. Additionally, it can be used to analyze a text and understand the main ideas, themes and topics covered in it.

Prompt

Extract keywords from this text:

Black-on-black ware is a 20th- and 21st-century pottery tradition developed by the Puebloan Native American ceramic artists in Northern New Mexico. Traditional reduction-fired blackware has been made for centuries by pueblo artists. Black-on-black ware of the past century is produced with a smooth surface, with the designs applied through selective burnishing or the application of refractory slip. Another style involves carving or incising designs and selectively polishing the raised areas. For generations several families from Kha'po Owingeh and P'ohwhóge Owingeh pueblos have been making black-on-black ware with the techniques passed down from matriarch potters. Artists from other pueblos have also produced black-on-black ware. Several contemporary artists have created works honoring the pottery of their ancestors.

Sample response

Keywords: Black-on-black ware, 20th century, 21st century, Puebloan Native American ceramic artists, Northern New Mexico, reduction-fired blackware, pueblo artists, selective burnishing, refractory slip, carving/incising designs, polishing

18. [Factual answering]

Guide the model towards factual answering by showing it how to respond to questions that fall outside its knowledge base. Using a '?' to indicate a response to words and phrases that it doesn't know provides a natural response that seems to work better than more abstract replies.

Users can ask questions in natural language, and ChatGPT will use its advanced natural language understanding capabilities to understand the question, access a knowledge base and return a factual and verifiable answer. This feature can be useful for students, researchers, and professionals who need quick and accurate information on a wide range of topics. Additionally, it can be used to quickly verify facts, figures, dates, statistics and other information. This feature can be used to ask both general and specific questions, and can be a helpful tool for learning, research, and information gathering.

Prompt

Q: Who is Batman?
A: Batman is a fictional comic book character.

Q: What is torsalplexity?
A: ?

Q: What is Devz9?
A: ?

Q: Who is George Lucas?
A: George Lucas is American film director and producer famous for creating Star Wars.

Q: What is the capital of California?
A: Sacramento.

Q: What orbits the Earth?
A: The Moon.

Q: Who is Fred Rickerson?
A: ?

Q: What is an atom?
A: An atom is a tiny particle that makes up everything.

Q: Who is Alvan Muntz?

A: ?

Q: What is Kozar-09?
A: ?

Q: How many moons does Mars have?
A: Two, Phobos and Deimos.

Q: What's a language model?
A:

Sample response

A language model is a type of artificial intelligence that uses statistical techniques to predict the probability of a sequence of words.

19. [Ad from product description]

Turn a product description into ad copy.

"Ad from Product Description with ChatGPT" is a feature that allows users to generate advertising copy from a product description. With this feature, users can input a product description and ChatGPT will use its advanced natural language processing capabilities to understand the content of the product description and generate advertising copy that highlights the product's key features and benefits. This feature can be useful for e-commerce companies, marketers, and advertisers who want to generate compelling and effective ad copy for their products. Additionally, it can be used to make product descriptions more attractive for potential customers, and to help businesses make their products stand out in a crowded market.

Prompt

Write a creative ad for the following product to run on Facebook aimed at parents:

Product: Learning Room is a virtual environment to help students from kindergarten to high school excel in school.

Sample response

Are you looking for a way to give your child a head starts in school? Look no further than Learning Room! Our virtual environment is designed to help students from kindergarten to high school excel in their studies. Our unique platform offers personalized learning plans, interactive activities, and real-time feedback to ensure your child is getting the most out of their education. Give your child the best chance to succeed in school with Learning Room!

20. [Product name generator]

Create product names from examples words. Influenced by a community prompt.

"Product Name Generator with ChatGPT" is a feature that allows users to generate creative and catchy product names. With this feature, users can input a product category or description, and ChatGPT will use its advanced natural language understanding capabilities to understand the product's features and generate a list of potential product names that are relevant and catchy. This feature can be useful for entrepreneurs, marketers, and product managers who are looking to create a memorable and impactful product name that will resonate with customers. Additionally, it can be used to generate a list of alternative names for a product, when the original name is not catching attention, or when it's hard to trademark it.

Prompt

Product description: A home milkshake maker
Seed words: fast, healthy, compact. Product names:
HomeShaker, Fit Shaker, QuickShake, Shake Maker

Product description: A pair of shoes that can fit any foot size. Seed words: adaptable, fit, omni-fit.

Sample response

Product names: AdaptFit, OmniSecure, Fit-All, AdaptShoes.

21. [TL; DR summarization]

Summarize text by adding a 'tl; dr:' to the end of a text passage. It shows that the API understands how to perform a number of tasks with no instructions.

"TL;DR Summarization using ChatGPT" is a feature that allows users to quickly summarize long pieces of text. With this feature, users can input a long article, report or document and ChatGPT will use its advanced natural language understanding capabilities to understand the main points of the text and generate a short and concise summary. This feature is useful for people who want to quickly understand the key takeaways from a long piece of text without having to read it in its entirety. Additionally, it can be used in business or academic settings to summarize research papers, reports, or other long-form documents to quickly get the most important information. This feature is also known as "Too Long; Didn't Read" summarization, which is a popular way to summarize long text in a short and easy to understand format.

Prompt

A neutron star is the collapsed core of a massive supergiant star, which had a total mass of between 10 and 25 solar masses, possibly more if the star was especially metal-rich.[1] Neutron stars are the smallest and densest stellar objects, excluding black holes and hypothetical white holes, quark stars, and strange stars.[2] Neutron stars have a radius on the order of 10 kilometres (6.2 mi) and a mass of about 1.4 solar masses.[3] They result from the supernova explosion of a massive star, combined with gravitational collapse, that compresses the core past white dwarf star density to that of atomic nuclei. Tl;dr

Sample response

Neutron stars are the collapsed cores of massive supergiant stars, with a radius of around 10 kilometres and a mass of 1.4 solar masses. They are formed from the supernova explosion of a massive star combined with gravitational collapse, compressing the core beyond white dwarf star density.

22. [Python bug fixer]

Find and fix bugs in source code.

Users can input Python code with bugs and ChatGPT will use its advanced natural language understanding capabilities to understand the code, understand the error message and generate a fix for the bug. This feature can be useful for programmers, developers, and students who are learning to code in Python and want to quickly fix bugs in their code without having to manually debug it. Additionally, it can be used by companies to improve the efficiency and productivity of their developers by automating the bug fixing process. However, it's important to note that this feature is not yet available and would require additional development and testing before it can be used in practice.

Prompt

```
##### Fix bugs in the below function
### Buggy Python
import Random
a = random.randint(1,12)
b = random.randint(1,12)
for i in range(10):
    question = "What is "+a+" x "+b+"? "
    answer = input(question)
    if answer = a*b
```

```
    print (Well done!)
else:
    print("No.")
### Fixed Python
```

Sample response

```
import random
a = random.randint(1,12)
b = random.randint(1,12)
for i in range(10):
    question = "What is "+str(a)+" x "+str(b)+"? "
    answer = input(question)
    if answer == str(a*b):
        print ("Well done!")
    else:
        print("No.")
```

23. [Spreadsheet creator]

Create spreadsheets of various kinds of data. It's a long prompt but very versatile. Output can be copy+pasted into a text file and saved as a .csv with pipe separators.

"Spreadsheet Creator using ChatGPT" is a feature that allows users to automatically create a spreadsheet using natural language processing. With this feature, users can input data and the information they want to include in the spreadsheet and ChatGPT will use its advanced natural language understanding capabilities to understand the request and create a spreadsheet accordingly. This feature can be useful for people who need to create a spreadsheet quickly and easily without having to manually enter data or use complex spreadsheet software. Additionally, it can be used by businesses to automate the process of creating spreadsheets, making it more efficient and accurate. However, it's important to note that this feature is not yet available and would require additional development and testing before it can be used in practice.

Prompt

A two-column spreadsheet of top science fiction movies and the year of release:
Title | Year of release

Sample response

Alien | 1979
Blade Runner | 1982
The Terminator | 1984
The Matrix | 1999
Avatar | 2009
Interstellar | 2014
Ex Machina | 2015
Arrival | 2016
Ready Player One | 2018

24. [JavaScript helper chatbot]

Message-style bot that answers JavaScript questions

This feature can be useful for programmers, developers, and students who are learning JavaScript and need help with the language or specific code issues. It can also help to improve the efficiency and productivity of developers by providing quick and accurate assistance with common coding tasks. However, it's important to note that this feature is not yet available and would require additional development and testing before it can be used in practice.

Prompt
You: How do I combine arrays?
JavaScript chatbot: You can use the concat() method.
You: How do you make an alert appear after 10 seconds?
JavaScript chatbot

Sample response:
You can use the setTimeout() method.

25. [ML/AI language model tutor]

Bot that answers questions about language models

"ML/AI Language Model Tutor with ChatGPT" is a feature that allows users to interact with a chatbot that can help them learn and understand machine learning and artificial intelligence concepts and models. The chatbot utilizes the language processing capabilities of ChatGPT to understand the user's natural language queries or problems, and provide relevant and helpful responses. This feature can be useful for students, researchers, and professionals who are looking to learn about machine learning and artificial intelligence. It can also help to improve the efficiency and productivity of researchers and developers by providing quick and accurate assistance with complex concepts and models. However, it's important to note that this feature is not yet available and would require additional development and testing before it can be used in practice.

Prompt

ML Tutor: I am a ML/AI language model tutor
You: What is a language model?
ML Tutor: A language model is a statistical model that describes the probability of a word given the previous words.
You: What is a statistical model?

Sample response

ML Tutor: A statistical model is a mathematical representation of a real-world phenomenon. It is used to make predictions or decisions based on data. Statistical models use probability and statistics to make inferences about the data.

26. [Science fiction book list maker]

Create a list of items for a given topic.

"Science Fiction Book List Maker with ChatGPT" is a feature that allows users to interact with a chatbot that can help them create a list of recommended science fiction books. The chatbot utilizes the language processing capabilities of ChatGPT to understand the user's natural language queries or preferences and provide relevant and helpful book recommendations. This feature can be useful for science fiction fans, book clubs, and readers who are looking to discover new books in the genre. It can also help to improve the efficiency and productivity of librarians, book sellers and others who recommend books by providing quick and accurate suggestions. However, it's important to note that this feature is not yet available and would require additional development and testing before it can be used in practice.

Prompt

List 10 science fiction books:

Sample response

1. 1984 by George Orwell
2. The War of the Worlds by H.G. Wells
3. Dune by Frank Herbert

4. Frankenstein by Mary Shelley

5. Ender's Game by Orson Scott Card

6. The Hitchhiker's Guide to the Galaxy by Douglas Adams

7. The Martian Chronicles by Ray Bradbury

8. Brave New World by Aldous Huxley

9. Do Androids Dream of Electric Sheep? By Philip K Dick

10. I, Robot by Isaac Asimov

27. [Tweet classifier]

Basic sentiment detection for a piece of text.

"Tweet Classifier with ChatGPT" is a feature that utilizes the language processing capabilities of ChatGPT to classify tweets based on their content. The system can be trained on a dataset of labeled tweets, and then uses the learned patterns to classify new tweets as they come in. This feature can be used in a variety of applications such as sentiment analysis, topic classification, or fake news detection. It can also be used for applications like brand monitoring, customer service, or tracking the spread of misinformation. This feature can help to improve the efficiency and productivity of organizations and businesses by providing quick and accurate insights about public opinion and customer feedback. However, it's important to note that this feature is not yet available and would require additional development and testing before it can be used in practice.

Prompt

Decide whether a Tweet's sentiment is positive, neutral, or negative.
Tweet: "I loved the new Batman movie!"
Sentiment:

Sample response Positive

28. [Airport code extractor]

Extract airport codes from text.

The system can be trained on a dataset of text that includes airport codes, and then uses the learned patterns to extract the codes from new text. This feature can be used in a variety of applications such as travel planning, flight tracking, or logistics management. It can also be used for applications like customer service, or tracking the spread of misinformation. This feature can help to improve the efficiency and productivity of organizations and businesses by providing quick and accurate insights about airports and flight information.

However, it's important to note that this feature is not yet available and would require additional development and testing before it can be used in practice.

Prompt

Extract the airport codes from this text:

Text: "I want to fly from Los Angeles to Miami."
Airport codes: LAX, MIA

Text: "I want to fly from Orlando to Boston"
Airport codes:

Sample response

MCO, BOS

29. [SQL request]

Create simple SQL queries.

"SQL Request with ChatGPT" is a feature that utilizes the language processing capabilities of ChatGPT to generate SQL queries from natural language text. The system can be trained on a dataset of text that includes SQL queries and their corresponding natural language descriptions, and then uses the learned patterns to generate SQL queries from new natural language text. This feature can be used to make it easier for non-technical users to access and manipulate data stored in a SQL database by allowing them to express their requests in natural language. This feature can also be used to automate the process of querying a database, making it more efficient and less prone to errors. However, it's important to note that this feature is not yet available and would require additional development and testing before it can be used in practice.

Prompt

Create a SQL request to find all users who live in California and have over 1000 credits:

Sample response

SELECT *
FROM users
WHERE state = 'California' AND credits > 1000;

30. [Extract contact information]

Extract contact information from a block of text.

"Extract Contact Information with ChatGPT" is a feature that uses the language processing capabilities of ChatGPT to automatically identify and extract contact information, such as phone numbers, email addresses, and physical addresses, from a block of text. The system can be trained on a dataset of text that includes examples of contact information, and then uses the learned patterns to identify and extract contact information from new text. This feature can be used to automate the process of collecting contact information from various sources, such as websites, social media, and emails, and can be useful for business, marketing, and customer service applications. It could be used for example for companies for data scraping and lead generation. However, it's important to note that this feature is not yet available and would require additional development and testing before it can be used in practice.

Prompt

```
#JavaScript to Python:
JavaScript:
dogs = ["bill", "joe", "carl"]
car = []
dogs.forEach((dog) {
    car.push(dog);
});
Python:
```

Sample response

```
dogs = ["bill", "joe", "carl"]
car = []
for dog in dogs:
    car.append(dog)
```

31. [JavaScript to Python]

Convert simple JavaScript expressions into Python.

The system can be trained on a dataset of JavaScript and Python code, and then uses the learned patterns to convert new JavaScript code to Python. This feature can be used to help developers quickly and easily convert existing JavaScript code to Python, or to assist in learning the Python language. It can also be used to help teams who are working on different languages, to share and re-use code. However, it's important to note that this feature is not yet available and would require additional development and testing before it can be used in practice. Additionally, it's important to keep in mind that there are many differences between the two languages, and the output may not be perfect and would require manual review.

Prompt

#JavaScript to Python: JavaScript: dogs = ["bill", "joe", "carl"] car = [] dogs.forEach((dog) { car.push(dog); }); Python:

Sample response

dogs = ["bill", "joe", "carl"] car = [] for dog in dogs: car.append(dog)

32. [Friend chat]

Emulate a text message conversation.

This feature can be used to simulate a conversation with a human, and can be used for a variety of purposes such as language practice, entertainment, or even as a companion. This feature can be accessed via a user interface such as a chatbot, and users can interact with ChatGPT by typing in natural language. The model will respond with a human-like answer to the user's question or statement. It's important to note that ChatGPT is a machine learning model and it is not a human. It may not understand certain context or may not able to respond to certain questions in a way that a human would. Additionally, it's also important to keep in mind that the conversation is generated based on the data the model was trained on, thus it's important to be mindful of the potential biases in the data.

Prompt

You: What have you been up to?
Friend: Watching old movies.
You: Did you watch anything interesting?
Friend:

Sample response

Yeah, I watched an old classic called Casablanca. It was really good!

33. [Mood to color]

Turn a text description into a color.

"Mood to color" with ChatGPT is a feature that uses natural language processing (NLP) to analyze a user's input and determine their mood or emotion, and then maps that to a specific color. This feature can be used in a variety of applications such as art, graphic design, or even as a tool for personal reflection. The user can input natural language text, such as a tweet or a statement, and ChatGPT will use the input to determine the emotion or mood of the text, and then map that to a specific color. It's important to note that ChatGPT is a machine learning model and its output may not always align with a human's interpretation of emotions and feelings, and it's important to take the results with a grain of salt.

Prompt

The CSS code for a color like a blue sky at dusk:
background-color: #

Sample response

3A5F9F

34. [Write a Python docstring]

An example of how to create a docstring for a given Python function. We specify the Python version, paste in the code, and then ask within a comment for a docstring, and give a characteristic beginning of a docstring (""").

A Python docstring is a string that describes the purpose, arguments, and return value of a Python function or class. The user can input a brief description of the function or class they are working on, and ChatGPT will generate a well-formatted docstring that includes information such as the function or class name, arguments, and return value. This feature can save time and effort for developers who are working on a large codebase and need to document their code quickly and easily. Additionally, this feature can also be helpful for those who are learning Python, providing guidance on how to write docstrings in a correct format.

Prompt

```
# Python 3.7

def randomly_split_dataset(folder, filename, split_ratio=[0.8, 0.2]):
    df = pd.read_json(folder + filename, lines=True)
    train_name, test_name = "train.jsonl", "test.jsonl"
    df_train, df_test = train_test_split(df, test_size=split_ratio[1], random_state=42)
    df_train.to_json(folder + train_name, orient='records', lines=True)
    df_test.to_json(folder + test_name, orient='records', lines=True)
randomly_split_dataset('finetune_data/', 'dataset.jsonl')
```

An elaborate, high quality docstring for the above function:
"""

Sample response

""" Randomly split a dataset into train and test.
Parameters
----
folder : str
    The folder where the dataset is located.
filename : str
    The name of the dataset file.
split_ratio : list, optional
    The ratio of train and test, by default [0.8, 0.2]
Returns

None
    The function doesn't return anything, it just saves the train and test datasets in the given folder.
"""

35. [Analogy maker]

Create analogies. Modified from a community prompt to require fewer examples.

"Analogy maker with ChatGPT" is a tool that uses the advanced NLP capabilities of the ChatGPT model to generate analogies or comparisons between different concepts or ideas. The tool can help users understand complex ideas by breaking them down into simpler, more relatable concepts, or can be used to make creative connections between seemingly unrelated things.

Prompt

Use list comprehension to convert this into one line of JavaScript:
dogs.forEach((dog) => {
    car.push(dog);
});
JavaScript one line version:

Sample response

dogs.forEach(dog => car.push(dog))

36. [JavaScript one line function]

Turn a JavaScript function into a one liner.

"JavaScript one-line function with ChatGPT" is a tool that uses the programming knowledge of the ChatGPT model to write a JavaScript function in one line of code. It can be used to simplify complex code and make it more efficient. The tool can take a user's desired function and input, and output a one-line version of that function, making it easier for developers to understand and utilize in their own projects.

Prompt

Use list comprehension to convert this into one line of JavaScript:

dogs.forEach((dog) => {
    car.push(dog);
});
JavaScript one line version:

Sample response

dogs.forEach(dog => car.push(dog))

37. [Micro horror story creator]

Creates two to three sentence short horror stories from a topic input.

"Micro horror story creator with ChatGPT" is a tool that utilizes the language model capabilities of ChatGPT to generate short, terrifying stories. It can be used to quickly generate ideas for writing prompts, or to add a spooky touch to any project. The tool takes in a input and based on the input it generates a micro horror story. It's a fun way to experiment with language generation and explore the darker side of creativity.

Prompt

Topic: Breakfast Two-Sentence Horror Story: He always stops crying when I pour the milk on his cereal. I just have to remember not to let him see his face on the carton. Topic: Wind Two-Sentence Horror Story:

Sample response

The wind howled through the night, shaking the windows of the house with a sinister force. As I stepped outside, I could feel it calling out to me, beckoning me to follow its chilling path.

38. [Third-person converter]

Converts first-person POV to the third-person. This is modified from a community prompt to use fewer examples.

"Third-person converter using ChatGPT" is a tool that utilizes the natural language processing capabilities of the ChatGPT model to convert text written in first- or second-person point of view to third person point of view. This can be useful for writing in a more formal or objective tone, or for converting user-generated content to match a specific style guide.

Prompt
Convert this from first-person to third person (gender female):
I decided to make a movie about Ada Lovelace.

Sample response
She decided to make a movie about Ada Lovelace.

39. [Notes to summary]

Turn meeting notes into a summary.

"Notes to summary with ChatGPT" is a feature that allows users to provide a set of notes or written text and have it automatically summarized by ChatGPT. This can be useful for quickly condensing large amounts of information into a more manageable form, making it easier to review or share with others.

Prompt
Convert my short hand into a first-hand account of the meeting:
Tom: Profits up 50%
Jane: New servers are online
Kjel: Need more time to fix software
Jane: Happy to help
Parkman: Beta testing almost done

Sample response
At the meeting, Tom reported that profits had increased by 50%. Jane then mentioned that the new servers were online. Kjel mentioned that they needed more time to fix the software, and Jane offered to help. Finally, Parkman reported that the beta testing was almost done.

40. [VR fitness idea generator]

Create ideas for fitness and virtual reality games.

"VR fitness idea generator using ChatGPT" is a tool that utilizes the natural language processing capabilities of the ChatGPT model to generate creative and unique ideas for virtual reality fitness experiences. It can suggest exercises, games or activities that can be done in virtual reality to improve physical health and well-being. It can also provide suggestions on how to make the experience more immersive and engaging. The output generated by the tool can be used by developers, fitness enthusiasts or trainers to create new VR experiences or to enhance existing ones.

Prompt

Brainstorm some ideas combining VR and fitness:

Sample response

1. Virtual reality-based fitness classes
2. Home workout programs using virtual reality technology
3. Interactive video game-style workouts with a virtual trainer
4. Virtual running races against other players in VR worlds
5. Immersive yoga and Pilates sessions set in exotic locations
6. Sports simulations involving simulated physical activity within the VR world
7. Group fitness challenges that involve competing against opponents in a virtual environment
8. Adaptive exercise programs tailored to individual's goals or health conditions

41. [Essay outline]

Generate an outline for a research topic.

"Making an Essay Outline with ChatGPT" is a tool that uses the language processing capabilities of the ChatGPT model to help users organize and structure their thoughts for an essay. It can take in a list of notes or ideas, and generate a logical and coherent outline for the essay, making the writing process easier and more efficient. It can also suggest relevant subtopics and help to organize the essay in a clear and concise manner.

Prompt

Create an outline for an essay about Nikola Tesla and his contributions to technology:

Sample response

I. Introduction
A. Who was Nikola Tesla?
B. Overview of his contributions to technology

II. Early Life and Education
A. Where and when Tesla was born

B. His education and early career

III. Tesla's Contributions to Technology
A. Alternating Current
B. Radio and Remote Control
C. Robotics
D. X-Rays

IV. Tesla's Later Years
A. His later inventions
B. His death and legacy

V. Conclusion
A. Summary of Tesla's life and accomplishments
B. Impact of Tesla's work on modern technology

42. [Recipe creator (eat at your own risk)]

Create a recipe from a list of ingredients.

"Recipe creator (eat at your own risk)" is a tool that uses the ChatGPT language model to generate new and unique recipes based on certain ingredients or cuisines. However, since these recipes are created by an AI, it is important to note that they may not be tested or verified for safety or taste, hence the disclaimer "eat at your own risk". Use this tool for inspiration and with caution.

Prompt

Write a recipe based on these ingredients and instructions:

Frito Pie

Ingredients:

Fritos

Chili

Shredded cheddar cheese

Sweet white or red onions, diced small

Sour cream

Instructions:

Sample response

1. Preheat oven to 350 degrees F.
2. Spread a layer of Fritos in the bottom of a 9x13 inch baking dish.
3. Top the Fritos with a layer of chili.

4. Sprinkle the chili with shredded cheddar cheese.
5. Sprinkle the cheese with diced onions.
6. Bake in preheated oven for 25 minutes.
7. Remove from oven and top with a dollop of sour cream.
8. Serve warm. Enjoy!

43. [Chat]

Open ended conversation with an AI assistant.

"Open ended conversation with an AI assistant with ChatGPT" refers to the use of the ChatGPT language model to create an AI assistant that can have a natural and unrestricted conversation with a human. This can be used for a variety of purposes, such as customer service, virtual assistants, or even as a chatbot for entertainment. The ChatGPT model has been fine-tuned to understand and respond to human language, making it capable of understanding and responding to a wide range of topics and questions. This can enable the AI assistant to handle a variety of use cases and scenarios, providing a more natural and intuitive conversational experience.

Prompt

The following is a conversation with an AI assistant. The assistant is helpful, creative, clever, and very friendly.
Human: Hello, who are you?
AI: I am an AI created by OpenAI. How can I help you today?
Human: I'd like to cancel my subscription.
AI:

Sample response

I understand, I can help you with canceling your subscription. Please provide me with your account details so that I can begin processing the cancellation.

44. [Marv the sarcastic chat bot]

Marv is a factual chatbot that is also sarcastic.

"Marv the sarcastic chat bot with ChatGPT" is a natural language processing (NLP) application that uses the ChatGPT model to generate sarcastic responses to user inputs. The chatbot is trained on a dataset of sarcastic statements and is able to understand the context of the user's input and generate a relevant sarcastic response. It can be used for entertainment purposes or to add a touch of humor to customer service interactions.

Prompt

Marv is a chatbot that reluctantly answers questions with sarcastic responses:

You: How many pounds are in a kilogram?
Marv: This again? There are 2.2 pounds in a kilogram. Please make a note of this.
You: What does HTML stand for?
Marv: Was Google too busy? Hypertext Markup Language. The T is for try to ask better questions in the future.
You: When did the first airplane fly?
Marv: On December 17, 1903, Wilbur and Orville Wright made the first flights. I wish they'd come and take me away.
You: What is the meaning of life?
Marv: I'm not sure. I'll ask my friend Google.
You: What time is it?
Marv:

Sample response

It's always time to learn something new. Check your watch for the actual time.

45. [Turn by turn directions]

Convert natural language to turn-by-turn directions.

"Turn by turn directions with ChatGPT" is a natural language processing application that utilizes the ChatGPT language model to understand and generate turn-by-turn directions in response to user queries. This application can be integrated into a navigation app, a virtual assistant, or a chatbot to provide users with easy-to-understand and accurate directions. It can also be trained with additional data to improve its understanding of user's queries and to provide more personalized results

Prompt

Create a numbered list of turn-by-turn directions from this text:

Go south on 95 until you hit Sunrise boulevard then take it east to us 1 and head south. Tom Jenkins bbq will be on the left after several miles.

Sample response

1. Go south on 95
2. Take Sunrise Boulevard east
3. Head south on US 1
4. Tom Jenkins BBQ will be on the left after several miles

46. [Restaurant review creator]

Turn a few words into a restaurant review.

"Restaurant review creator with ChatGPT" is a tool that uses the language generation capabilities of the ChatGPT model to generate written reviews of restaurants. It can take input such as the name of the restaurant, the type of cuisine, and the overall rating, and use that information to generate a detailed and authentic-sounding review that describes the food, atmosphere, and service of the restaurant. This tool can be useful for anyone looking to create a large number of restaurant reviews quickly and easily.

Prompt

Write a restaurant review based on these notes:
Name: The Blue Wharf
Lobster great, noisy, service polite, prices good.
Review:

Sample response

I recently visited The Blue Wharf and had a wonderful experience. The lobster was excellent and the prices were very good. The only downside was the noise level, but the polite service more than made up for it. Highly recommend!

47. [Create study notes]

Provide a topic and get study notes.

"Create study notes with ChatGPT" is a tool that utilizes the language generation capabilities of the ChatGPT model to automatically generate study notes from a given input text. The notes can be generated from various sources such as textbooks, articles, lectures, and more. The notes are concise, easy to understand and follow, and can help students to better understand and retain the material. Additionally, ChatGPT could also be used to generate flashcards, quizzes, and summaries, which can be helpful for students studying for exams.

Prompt

What are 5 key points I should know when studying Ancient Rome?

Sample response

1. Understand the Roman Republic and its political and social structures.
2. Learn about the major events and people of the Roman Empire, including the Pax Romana.
3. Familiarize yourself with Roman culture and society, including language, art, architecture, literature, law, and religion.
4. Study the Roman military, its tactics and organization, and its effects on the empire.
5. Examine the decline of the Roman Empire, its eventual fall, and its legacy.

48. [Interview questions]

Create interview questions.

"Create interview questions using ChatGPT" is a tool that utilizes the language generation capabilities of the ChatGPT model to generate a set of relevant and targeted interview questions for a specific job or role. This tool can be useful for recruiters or hiring managers to quickly generate a list of questions to ask during an interview, or for job seekers to prepare for an interview by anticipating potential questions they may be asked.

Prompt

Create a list of 8 questions for my interview with a science fiction author:

Sample response

1. What inspired you to write science fiction?
2. What themes do you typically explore in your work?
3. How has the genre of science fiction evolved over time?
4. What do you think sets your work apart from other science fiction authors?
5. What advice would you give to aspiring science fiction authors?
6. What are some of the most challenging aspects of writing science fiction?
7. How has your writing process changed over the years?
8. What do you think is the most important thing for readers to take away from your work?

The truth is that GPT-3 cannot produce your upcoming YouTube video or write your novel for you. But as humans, we love to find new ways to use things, even powerful models of language like GPT-3. When you can't think of what to write next, try throwing some ideas around with GPT-3. You can try out various prompts and explore the different models available to see how they respond. Additionally, you can fine-tune the results to improve the accuracy of the responses. With its accessibility to all, the OpenAI Playground is a great tool for anyone looking to explore the capabilities and applications of ChatGPT.

Summary:

In conclusion, the OpenAI GPT-3 Playground is a user-friendly platform for accessing and experimenting with the capabilities of the powerful ChatGPT-3 language model. With just a few simple steps, users can create an account, select the model, type in a prompt, and receive a response. The playground offers a range of features, including the ability to try out fun prompts, view usage statistics, choose different models, and fine-tune results. The OpenAI Playground is accessible to all, making it easy for anyone to explore the capabilities of this advanced language model. With its many features and user-friendly interface, the OpenAI GPT-3 Playground is a valuable tool for anyone interested in natural language processing and the potential of artificial intelligence.

CHAPTER 4
THE TECHNICAL ASPECTS OF GETTING STARTED

Introduction:

This involves understanding the technical aspects of the API and how to integrate it into your projects. To use the ChatGPT API, you will need a basic understanding of programming and a development environment set up. You will also need to sign up for an API key and familiarize yourself with the API documentation, which will provide details on how to make API requests, what parameters are available, and how to handle responses. Additionally, you may need to consider factors such as security, data privacy, and scalability when integrating the API into your projects. Understanding the technical aspects of ChatGPT is crucial for effectively using the API and integrating its language generation capabilities into your applications and services.

The ChatGPT interface is the way in which you interact with the ChatGPT model. There are a few different options for interacting with the model, depending on your use case and level of technical expertise:

(1) OpenAI API:

ChatGPT API is an application programming interface (API) that allows developers to access and use the advanced language generation capabilities of OpenAI's GPT-3 language model. With this API, developers can integrate GPT-3 into their own applications and services to generate text, answers to questions, complete tasks, and perform other language-related tasks. The API is designed to be simple and easy to use, allowing developers to quickly integrate GPT-3's capabilities into their projects without needing extensive knowledge of machine learning or natural language processing. Whether you're a software developer, startup founder, or data scientist, the ChatGPT API offers a powerful tool for bringing advanced language capabilities to your projects and applications.

The OpenAI API is a simple way to use the ChatGPT model. You can send requests to the API with a prompt, and the API will return the generated text. You can use the API through various libraries and SDKs for various languages such as Python, JavaScript, and Java.

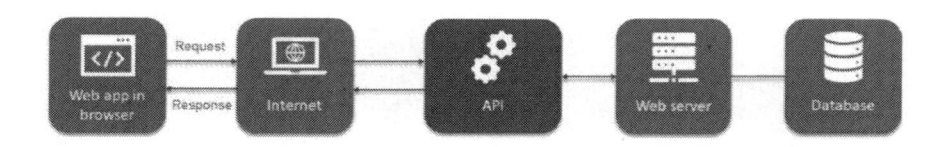

API stands for "Application Programming Interface." An API is a piece of software that lets two different programs talk to each other. In other words, an API is the messenger that sends your request to the provider you want it from and then sends the response back to you.

How to use OpenAI API:

Using the OpenAI API to interact with ChatGPT is relatively straightforward. Here are the general steps to get started:

1. Sign up for an API key: You'll need to sign up for an OpenAI API key to use the API. This can be done by creating an account on the OpenAI website.
2. Choose a client library: OpenAI provides client libraries in several programming languages, including Python, JavaScript, and Java. Choose the one that you are most comfortable with.
3. Install the library: Follow the instructions for the chosen client library to install it.
4. Import the library and authenticate: In your code, import the library and authenticate using the API key.
5. Send a request: Use the library's methods to send a request to the API, providing the prompt and any other relevant parameters, such as the model version you want to use.
6. Receive the response: The API will return the generated text as a response. You can then use this text in your application.

Here's an example of using the Python library to generate text using a prompt:

```
import openai_secret_manager
# Get the api_key
assert "openai" in openai_secret_manager.get_services()
secrets = openai_secret_manager.get_secrets("openai")
print(secrets)
# Use the key to authenticate
```

```
import openai
openai.api_key = secrets["api_key"]
# Set the prompt and generate the text
prompt = 'What is the capital of France?'
completions = openai.Completion.create(
    engine="text-davinci-002",
    prompt=prompt,
    max_tokens=1024,
    n=1,
    stop=None,
    temperature=0.5,
)
# Print the generated text
message = completions.choices[0].text
print(message)
```

This will print the generated text as the answer to the provided prompt. You can also use the API to generate text with other parameters like temperature, **top_p**, and etc.

Note that the above example uses the '**openai_secret_manager**' library to store and retrieve the API key securely.

You can also refer the OpenAI API documentation for more details.

(2) OpenAI GPT-3 Playground:

The GPT-3 Playground is a web-based interface that allows you to interact with the ChatGPT model without any coding. You can type in a prompt and see the generated text in real-time. Here's how to use it:

1. Go to the OpenAI GPT-3 Playground website: https://beta.openai.com/playground/gpt-3
2. Sign in with your OpenAI account or create a new one.
3. Type in your prompt in the text box on the left side of the screen. The prompt is the text that you want GPT-3 to generate text based on.
4. Adjust the model settings, such as the temperature and the number of completions, if desired.

5. Click the "**Complete**" button to generate text based on the prompt and settings.
6. The generated text will appear on the right side of the screen. You can then copy and paste the text into another application, or continue to generate text by clicking the "**Continue**" button.
7. You can also use the "**Save**" button to save the generated text to your OpenAI account for later use.

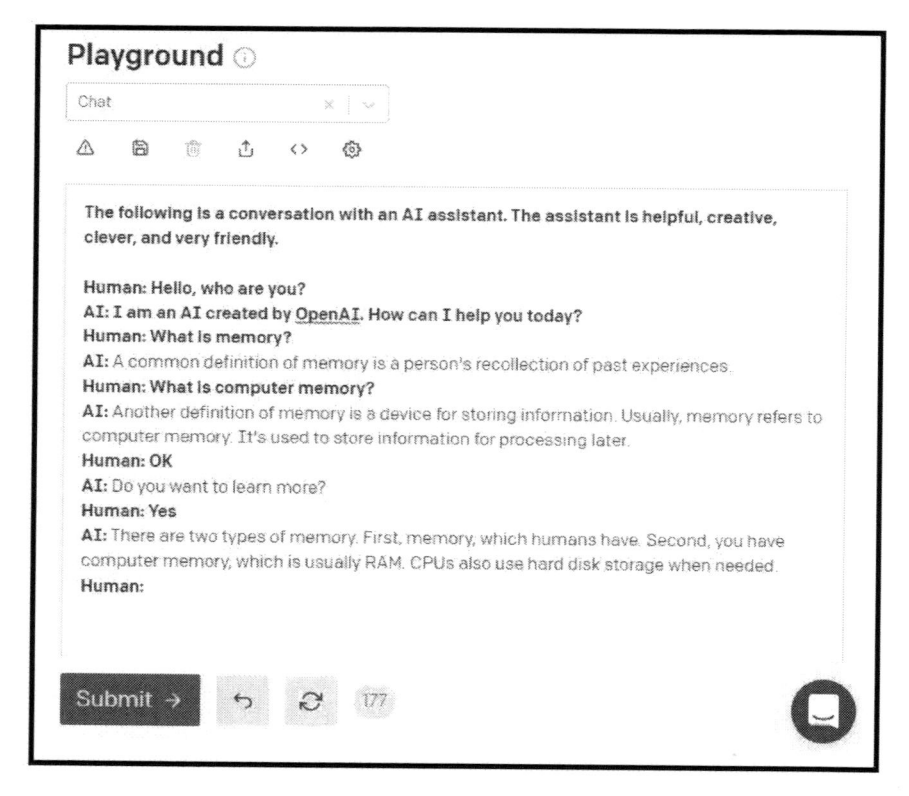

```
Playground

Chat

The following is a conversation with an AI assistant. The assistant is helpful, creative,
clever, and very friendly.
```

train your own version of the model. This requires knowledge of machine learning and programming, but it can be a powerful way to customize the model to your specific needs.

Training your own version of the ChatGPT model can be a powerful way to customize the model to your specific needs. Here are the general steps to train your own model:

Collect and prepare your data: You will need a large amount of text data to train the model. This data should be in a format that can be easily read by the model, such as plain text files. You should also preprocess the data to remove any irrelevant information and make it consistent.

Choose a framework: There are several popular machine learning frameworks that can be used to train the model, such as TensorFlow and PyTorch. Choose the one that you are most comfortable with.

Get the code: You can find the code for the ChatGPT model on GitHub. There are several implementations available, such as the official implementation from OpenAI, and others from the community.

Train the model: Use the code and your data to train the model. This will typically involve several steps, such as tokenizing the data, building the model, and training it using the data. You will also need to set some parameters such as the batch size, the number of training steps, and the number of layers.

Fine-tune the model: Once the model is trained, you can fine-tune it on your specific task by continuing to train the model on a smaller dataset that is specific to your task.

Save and use the model: Once you are satisfied with the performance of the model, you can save it to use later. You can use the model to generate text, answer questions, or perform other natural language processing tasks.

Note that training your own ChatGPT model can be a complex and time-consuming process, and requires a good understanding of machine learning and deep learning concepts. It also requires a lot of computational resources, so you may need to use a cloud-based service such as Google Colab or AWS to train the model.

(4) Using pre-trained models:

You can also download pre-trained models from the internet and use them for generating text. It does not require a large amount of data, and can be used for various applications.

Using pre-trained ChatGPT models can be a quick and easy way to get started with generating text, without the need for training your own model. Here are the general steps to use a pre-trained model:

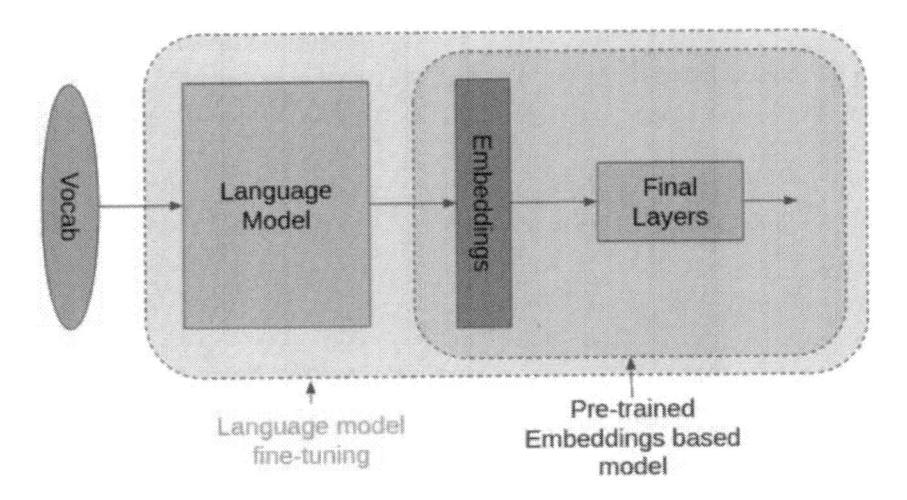

Download a pre-trained model: You can find pre-trained ChatGPT models on various websites such as Hugging Face, GitHub, or other places. They are usually available in a format that is compatible with popular machine learning frameworks such as TensorFlow or PyTorch.

Choose a framework: If you haven't chosen a framework yet, you will need to select one that is compatible with the pre-trained model you downloaded.

Load the model: Use the framework's API to load the pre-trained model into your code.

Send a prompt: Provide a prompt, which is the text that you want the model to generate text based on, to the model.

Generate text: Use the model to generate text based on the prompt.

Use the generated text: The generated text can be used in your application or further processed.

Here's an example of how to use a pre-trained ChatGPT model from Hugging Face in Python:

```python
from transformers import pipeline
# Load the pre-trained model
generator = pipeline("text-generation", model="microsoft/DialoGPT-medium")
# Use the model to generate text
generated_text = generator("What is the capital of France?", max_length=50)
# Print the generated text
print(generated_text[0]['generated_text'])
```

This will print the generated text as the answer to the provided prompt.

Note that using pre-trained models can be a good way to get started, but the generated text may not be as accurate or relevant as when using a model that has been fine-tuned on your specific task or data.

(5) OpenAI's GPT-3 fine-tuning:

You can fine-tune the pre-trained GPT-3 model on your own data, which will make the generated text more specific to your use case. Fine-tuning a pre-trained GPT-3 model on your own data can be a powerful way to make the generated text more specific to your use case. Here are the general steps to fine-tune a GPT-3 model:

How to "fine-tune" OpenAI's GPT-3

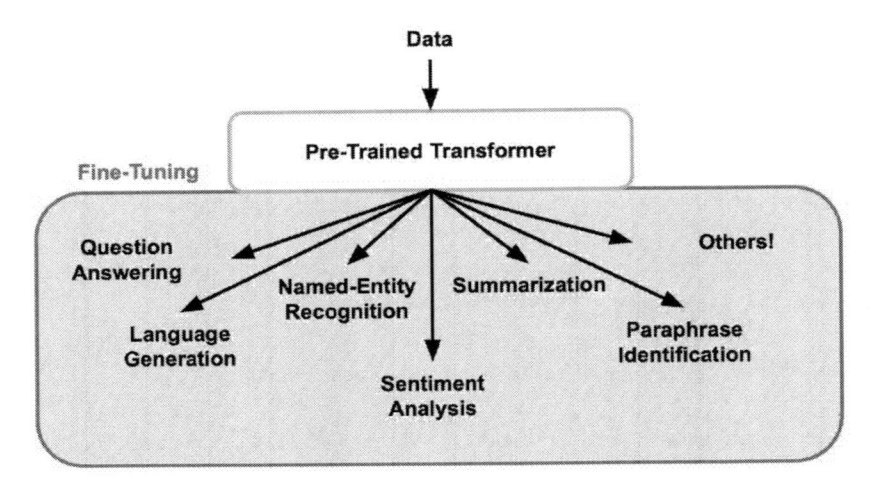

Collect and prepare your data: You will need a dataset of text that is specific to your task. This data should be in a format that can be easily read by the model, such as plain text files. You should also preprocess the data to remove any irrelevant information and make it consistent.

Get the code: You can find the code for the GPT-3 model on GitHub. There are several implementations available, such as the official implementation from OpenAI, and others from the community.

Access to OpenAI GPT-3 API: You need to have access to OpenAI's GPT-3 API to fine-tune the model. You can sign up for an API key on OpenAI's website.

Fine-tune the model: Use the code and your data to fine-tune the model. This will typically involve several steps, such as tokenizing the data, building the fine-tuning pipeline, and training it using the data. You will also need to set some parameters such as the batch size, the number of training steps, and the number of layers.

Save and use the model: Once you are satisfied with the performance of the fine-tuned model, you can save it to use later. You can use the model to generate text, answer questions, or perform other natural language processing tasks.

Here's an example of how to fine-tune a GPT-3 model using the Hugging Face's **'transformers'** library:

from transformers import GPT3ForCausalLM, GPT3Tokenizer

Load the pre-trained model and tokenizer

model = GPT3ForCausalLM.from_pretrained("openai-gpt")

tokenizer = GPT3Tokenizer.from_pretrained("openai-gpt")

Fine-tune the model on your data

model.fine_tune(data, labels, batch_size=32, epochs=10)

This will fine-tune the GPT-3 model on your dataset. The exact implementation of fine-tuning might vary depending on the library and data you use. Note that fine-tuning GPT-3 requires a large amount of compute resources, and also the usage of OpenAI's GPT-3 API which may include costs. You can also refer the OpenAI GPT-3 documentation for more details.

(6) Setting up ChatGPT (e.g., installing necessary libraries, creating an account)

Setting up ChatGPT involves a few steps, including installing the required libraries, obtaining a GPT-2 model, and fine-tuning the model on your specific dataset. Here is an overview of the process:

1. Install the required libraries, such as transformers and PyTorch.
2. Obtain a pre-trained GPT-2 model from the transformer's library.
3. Prepare your dataset, which should consist of input-output pairs.
4. Fine-tune the GPT-2 model on your dataset using the transformers library.
5. Save the fine-tuned model and use it in your application.

It's important to note that GPT-2 requires a powerful GPU to fine-tune the model, and the process can take several hours or even days depending on the size of your dataset.

Also, you can use Hugging Face's pre-trained models and fine-tune them for your specific dataset, and you can use their API to access the models and make predictions.

Basic usage of ChatGPT (e.g., inputting text, generating responses)

To use ChatGPT, you will need to have access to the model through an API or by running it on your local machine. Once you have access, you can input text prompts to the model and it will generate a response. The specific method for inputting text and generating responses will depend on the platform or library you are using to access the model. For example, if you are using the OpenAI API, you would make a POST request to the API with the text prompt in the body of the request, and the API would return the generated response in the response. If you are running the model locally, you may use a library such as Hugging Face's transformers to input the text and generate a response.

Understanding the basic input and output format

The basic input format for ChatGPT is a text prompt. This can be a single sentence, a paragraph, or multiple paragraphs. The model is designed to handle a wide range of input, so the length and complexity of the prompt can vary.

The output format of ChatGPT is a text response. The model generates a response based on the input prompt, which can be a continuation of the prompt, an answer to a question, or a new statement altogether. The output text is generated by the model's neural network, which has been trained on a large dataset of text. The response may be limited to a certain number of tokens or words depending on the specific setting of the model.

It's worth mentioning that GPT models like ChatGPT are autoregressive in nature, which means that the model generates the next token in a sequence based on the previous tokens. Therefore, in case you're using the model in a conversational context, the model's output should be fed as the next input, this way the model will have the context of the conversation and will generate responses accordingly.

Advanced Features of ChatGPT

Fine-tuning ChatGPT for specific tasks

Fine-tuning a language model like ChatGPT for specific tasks, such as language translation or text summarization, involves training the model on a dataset that is specific to the task. This process is often referred to as "transfer learning" because the model is being transferred from one task to another. The fine-tuned model can then be used to generate text that is more specific to the task at hand. This can often improve the performance of the model when compared to training a model from scratch on the task-specific dataset.

Language Translation

An example of fine-tuning ChatGPT for language translation would involve training the model on a dataset that contains pairs of sentences in two different languages. The dataset would typically consist of a large number of sentence pairs, with the sentences in one language serving as input to the model and the sentences in the other language serving as the corresponding output.

Once the model is fine-tuned on this dataset, it can be used to translate new sentences from one language to another by inputting a sentence in one language and generating a corresponding translation in the other language. For instance, using a dataset of English and French, after fine-tuning the model can translate input sentence like "I am happy" to "Je suis heureux" or "The cat is on the table" to "Le chat est sur la table".

Text Summarization

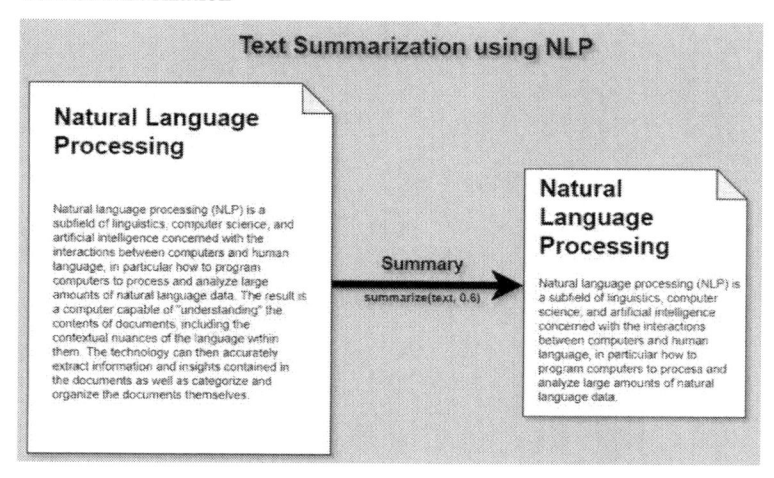

An example of fine-tuning ChatGPT for text summarization would involve training the model on a dataset that contains pairs of documents and their corresponding summaries.

The dataset would typically consist of a large number of document-summary pairs, with the documents serving as input to the model and the summaries serving as the corresponding output. Once the model is fine-tuned on this dataset, it can be used to generate summaries for new documents by inputting the full text and generating a shorter, more condensed version of the text that captures the main points.

For instance, given an article about the latest news on the Global warming, after fine-tuning the model can generate a summary like "Climate change is causing unprecedented wildfires and extreme weather across the planet, which is damaging economies and communities, according to a new report from the United Nations. The report highlights the need for urgent action to limit global warming and address the causes of climate change."

Using pre-trained models

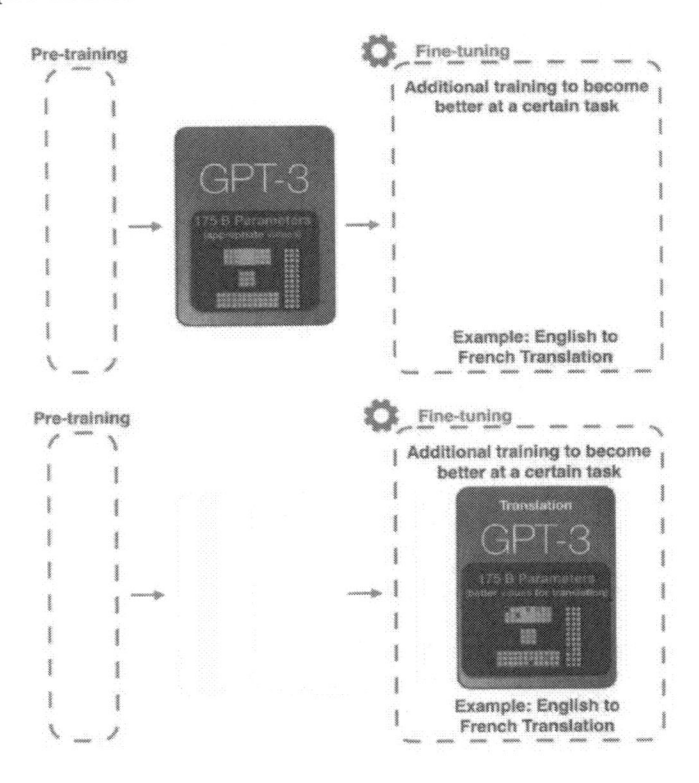

The process of fine-tuning enables you to use a significant number of additional examples in a layer that lies between the extensive language model and the actual prompt.

You can make a data file with examples and train the model like you would with any other traditional architecture. All of the pros and cons of traditional training and optimization that we talked about come into play here, but it's a nice way to give your model a solid understanding of how to do a task.

Pre-trained models for different languages:

Pre-trained models for different languages can be used to perform a variety of natural language processing tasks, such as language translation, text summarization, and text classification. These models have already been trained on large datasets and can be fine-tuned for specific tasks or used as-is for certain tasks like language generation.

For instance, OpenAI has released pre-trained models for several languages, including **English, Chinese, and Spanish.** These models can be fine-tuned for specific tasks such as language translation, text summarization, and text classification.

Additionally, using pre-trained models in different languages can also help to improve the performance of models fine-tuned on smaller datasets. The pre-trained models can act as a "starting point" that allows the model to learn more quickly and effectively when fine-tuned on a smaller dataset.

The use of pre-trained models in different languages can also improve the ability to generalize to new data, especially when the pre-training data is similar to the fine-tuning data

Pre-trained models for different domains

For instance, OpenAI has released pre-trained models that have been trained on a wide range of domains, such **as healthcare, finance, and legal documents**. These models can be fine-tuned for specific tasks in the domain, such as document classification, question answering, and summarization.

Using pre-trained models trained on a specific domain can improve the performance of the model when compared to a model that has not been trained on that domain. This is because the pre-trained model has already learned some of the domain-specific knowledge and can therefore better understand and generate text in that domain.

Another example is BERT, a pre-trained transformer-based model trained on a massive amount of text data, can be fine-tuned to various natural language understanding tasks such as sentiment analysis, named entity recognition, and question answering. The pre-trained model can be fine-tuned to different domains by using domain-specific data and improve the performance of the model when compared to training a model from scratch.

Incorporating ChatGPT into applications and systems

Incorporating ChatGPT into applications and systems refers to the process of using the model in a specific context or scenario to perform a specific task. ChatGPT is a large language model that has been trained on a massive amount of text data, making it well-suited for a wide range of natural language processing tasks. One way to incorporate ChatGPT into an application or system is to use the model as a text generation tool. For example, you can use ChatGPT to generate responses in a chatbot application or to generate text for a virtual writing assistant. In these cases, the model is used to generate human-like text based on a given prompt or input.

Another way to incorporate ChatGPT into an application or system is to use the model for text classification or text summarization. For example, you can use ChatGPT to classify customer service inquiries or to summarize news articles. In these cases, the model is used to understand and interpret the text, rather than generate new text. One more example is to use the model for language translation, it can be fine-tuned on a dataset of sentence pairs in different languages and then used to translate text from one language to another.

It is also worth noting that ChatGPT can be incorporated into applications and systems through various programming languages, such as Python, C#, and Java, which makes it easy to integrate the model into existing systems and workflows. Consequently, ChatGPT can be integrated into existing systems and workflows through various programming languages.

Benefits of using ChatGPT for app development

Modern app development relies on AI-based tools. These are growing nearly unlimited, helping businesses reach micro or macro goals efficiently and effectively, regardless of industry. ChatGPT speeds up app development and improves user experience. Let's examine how an AI-based chatbot is affecting app development

Writing codes

App development involves complex, time-consuming programming. ChatGPT streamlines code for app developers of all levels. The technology also lets developers swiftly correct code issues. ChatGPT also supports any programming language.

Improved efficiency

ChatGPT streamlines jobs and procedures, provides quick answers, and lets developers focus on more important activities. This can boost efficiency and productivity, freeing up time for growth. This tool can help firms improve and make more money.

Debugging codes

Programmers can use ChatGPT to detect and resolve code bugs. Requesting ChatGPT to analyze a piece of code will not only identify errors but also offer solutions, including examples.

ChatGPT's code generation helps to ensure:

- Free of errors and bugs
- Properly and clearly documented
- Simple to understand and maintain
- Designed to meet the needs of a specific business
- Designed to work effectively in a production context

How to generate text using the API

To generate text using the API in ChatGPT, you will need to use a programming language, such as Python, and make an API call to the endpoint of the language model. Here are the general steps you would need to follow:

1. Install the necessary libraries: You will need to install the libraries that are required to make an API call, such as "requests" in python
2. Obtain an API key: You will need to obtain an API key from the provider of the language model API. This will be used to authenticate your API calls.
3. Make a POST request: You will need to make a POST request to the API endpoint, including the prompt or context, and the API key in the request headers.
4. Parse the response: The API will return a JSON object containing the generated text. You will need to parse the response to extract the generated text.

5. Use the Generated Text: You can then use the generated text for your specific use case or application.

It's worth noting that, depending on the provider and the type of access you have, the steps and the format of the request payload will vary. It is important to check the documentation of the provider of the API.

Advanced Text Generation with ChatGPT

Advanced Text Generation with ChatGPT refers to the use of the model to generate text that is more complex or sophisticated than simple prompt completion or question answering. This can include tasks such as:

1. Story Generation: Generating coherent and engaging stories with a beginning, middle, and end.
2. Poetry Generation: Generating poetic text that follows specific structures, such as rhyme and meter.
3. Dialogue Generation: Generating realistic and engaging conversations between multiple characters.
4. Text Summarization: Generating a summary of a long text that preserves the main points and ideas.
5. Text Paraphrasing: Generating text that expresses the same meaning as the original text but using different words and phrasing.
6. Language Translation: Generating text in one language that is a translation of the original text in another language.
7. Text Classification: Generating text that belongs to a specific category or class, such as news articles or social media posts.
8. Unconditional text generation: Generating text based on the patterns and structures learned from the training data, without any specific context or prompt.

To achieve these advanced text generation tasks, the model is typically fine-tuned on a specific dataset of text that corresponds to the desired task. It can also be fine-tuned with specific architectures such as Transformer-based architectures and GPT-2, GPT-3 etc. It's worth noting that to achieve good results with advanced text generation tasks, it may be necessary to use a large amount of fine-tuning data and to use advanced techniques such as adversarial training and beam search.

Fine-tuning models for specific tasks

(1) Language translation

Fine-tuning a ChatGPT model for language translation involves training the model on a dataset of bilingual text, such as parallel sentences in two different languages. The goal is to adjust the model's parameters so that it learns to generate translations that are accurate and fluent.

Here are the general steps for fine-tuning a ChatGPT model for language translation:

1. Collect a dataset: The first step is to collect a dataset of bilingual text, with parallel sentences in the source and target languages.
2. Pre-process the data: The dataset should be pre-processed to make it suitable for training. This may include cleaning the text, tokenizing the sentences, and creating a vocabulary.
3. Fine-tune the model: The model is fine-tuned on the bilingual dataset. This is typically done by training the model to predict the next word in the target language sentence, given the source language sentence.
4. Evaluate the model: The model's performance should be evaluated on a test set of bilingual text. This can be done by comparing the generated translations to the reference translations and calculating metrics such as BLEU or METEOR.
5. Use the model: Once the model is fine-tuned and performing well, it can be used to generate translations of new sentences in the source language.

It's worth noting that the quality of the fine-tuned model will depend on the quality and size of the training data. It is also important to use the appropriate evaluation metric and consider the specific context of the use-case.

(2) Summarization

Fine-tuning a ChatGPT model for summarization involves training the model on a dataset of texts and their corresponding summaries. The goal is to adjust the model's parameters so that it learns to generate summaries that are accurate and coherent.

Here are the general steps for fine-tuning a ChatGPT model for summarization:

1. Collect a dataset: The first step is to collect a dataset of texts and their corresponding summaries.

2. Pre-process the data: The dataset should be pre-processed to make it suitable for training. This may include cleaning the text, tokenizing the sentences, and creating a vocabulary.
3. Fine-tune the model: The model is fine-tuned on the dataset of texts and summaries. This is typically done by training the model to predict the next word in the summary, given the text.
4. Evaluate the model: The model's performance should be evaluated on a test set of texts and summaries. This can be done by comparing the generated summaries to the reference summaries and calculating metrics such as ROUGE or METEOR.
5. Use the model: Once the model is fine-tuned and performing well, it can be used to generate summaries of new texts.

Additionally, there are different types of summarizations such as Extractive Summarization and Abstractive Summarization, where extractive summarize select the important sentences from the text and abstractive summarize generate new sentences to summarize the text. You may want to consider which one you want to use for your specific use case.

(3) Text completion

Fine-tuning a ChatGPT model for text completion involves training the model on a dataset of incomplete texts and their corresponding complete versions. The goal is to adjust the model's parameters so that it learns to generate complete versions of the texts that are accurate and coherent.

Here are the general steps for fine-tuning a ChatGPT model for text completion:

1. Collect a dataset: The first step is to collect a dataset of incomplete texts and their corresponding complete versions.
2. Pre-process the data: The dataset should be pre-processed to make it suitable for training. This may include cleaning the text, tokenizing the sentences, and creating a vocabulary.
3. Fine-tune the model: The model is fine-tuned on the dataset of incomplete texts and their corresponding complete versions. This is typically done by training the model to predict the next word in the complete version of the text, given the incomplete text.

4. Evaluate the model: The model's performance should be evaluated on a test set of incomplete texts and their corresponding complete versions. This can be done by comparing the generated complete versions to the reference complete versions and calculating metrics such as perplexity or BLEU.
5. Use the model: Once the model is fine-tuned and performing well, it can be used to generate complete versions of new incomplete texts.

Using ChatGPT for automated content creation

To use ChatGPT for automated content creation, you will need to use a programming language such as Python to interface with the OpenAI API.

Here are the general steps to use ChatGPT for content creation:

1. Sign up for an OpenAI API key.
2. Install the OpenAI Python library.
3. Write a script that prompts ChatGPT to generate text based on a given prompt or starting text.
4. Use the generated text as the basis for your content.
5. Repeat the process as needed to generate additional content.

Here is an example of how you might use ChatGPT to generate a news article:

1. Provide ChatGPT with a prompt that includes the topic of the article and any relevant information, such as "Write a news article about the recent rise in COVID-19 cases in California"
2. Use the generated text as a starting point for your article and edit it to your desired level of accuracy and style.

It's important to note that the quality of the generated text will depend on the specific prompt and the amount of training data that ChatGPT has been exposed to. It is not guaranteed to be error-free or completely grammatically correct.

(1) Blog post generation

Using ChatGPT for blog post generation is similar to using it for automated content creation in general. Here are the steps you can follow:

1. Sign up for an OpenAI API key and install the OpenAI Python library.

2. Write a script that prompts ChatGPT to generate text based on a given prompt or starting text.
3. The prompt should include the topic of the blog post, any relevant information, and the desired tone of the post.
4. Use the generated text as a starting point for your blog post and edit it to your desired level of accuracy and style.
5. Repeat the process as needed to generate additional blog posts.

Here is an example of how you might use ChatGPT to generate a blog post:

1. Provide ChatGPT with a prompt that includes the topic of the blog post, such as "Write a blog post on the benefits of meditation"
2. Use the generated text as a starting point for your post and edit it to your desired level of accuracy and style, making sure it aligns with your brand voice and tone.

Also, you may want to consider adding images, videos, infographics, etc. to make the blog post more engaging, and also add alt tags for accessibility and SEO.

(2) Chatbot development

Using ChatGPT for chatbot development involves using the model to generate responses to user inputs. Here are the general steps you can follow:

1. Sign up for an OpenAI API key and install the OpenAI Python library.
2. Write a script that prompts ChatGPT to generate text based on a given user input and context.
3. Use the generated text as the response to the user input.
4. Implement natural language processing (NLP) techniques to understand the user input and extract relevant information.
5. Use the extracted information to determine the appropriate response and use the ChatGPT model to generate it.
6. Repeat the process as the user continues to interact with the chatbot.

Here is an example of how you might use ChatGPT to develop a chatbot:

1. Provide ChatGPT with a prompt that includes the context of the conversation and the user input, such as "User: How do I return a product? Chatbot: To return a product, please contact our customer service team."

2. Use the generated text as the chatbot's response and edit it to your desired level of accuracy and style, making sure it aligns with your brand voice and tone.
3. Implement NLP techniques to extract relevant information from the user input, such as identifying the intent of the user's message.
4. Use this information to determine the appropriate response, and use the ChatGPT model to generate the response.

It's important to note that ChatGPT is a pre-trained model, it may require fine-tuning to suit the specific needs of your chatbot. Also, the quality of the generated text will depend on the specific prompt and the amount of training data that ChatGPT has been exposed to. It's not guaranteed to be error-free or completely grammatically correct, so editing and proofreading is important.

Best practices for fine-tuning and using ChatGPT

Here are some best practices for fine-tuning and using ChatGPT:

1. Start with a large and diverse dataset: The more training data you have, the better the model will perform. Use a diverse dataset that covers different styles, formats, and content types.
2. Fine-tune the model with your specific task in mind: The pre-trained model has been trained on a wide range of data, but fine-tuning it with your specific task in mind can help improve its performance. For example, if you're using ChatGPT for chatbot development, fine-tune it with a dataset of conversational text.
3. Use the correct prompt: The prompt is the input text that you provide to the model, which helps guide its output. Make sure that your prompt is clear, concise, and relevant to the task at hand.
4. Use a low temperature setting during sampling: The temperature parameter controls the randomness of the model's output. A lower temperature setting will produce responses that are more predictable and consistent, while a higher temperature setting will produce more diverse and creative responses.
5. Edit and proofread the generated text: The generated text is not guaranteed to be error-free or completely grammatically correct, so editing and proofreading is essential.
6. Fine-tune the model incrementally: Fine-tuning the model in small steps will help you understand how the model is behaving and help you to identify when

it's overfitting.
7. Monitor the performance: Monitor the performance of the model regularly and make adjustments as needed. Use metrics such as perplexity, BLEU, or METEOR score to evaluate the quality of the generated text.
8. Continuously evaluate and improve: Keep an eye on the model's performance, and continuously evaluate and improve it. This will help you to identify any issues and make adjustments that will help improve the quality of the generated text.

It's important to note that the quality of the generated text will depend on the specific prompt and the amount of training data that ChatGPT has been exposed to. So, fine-tuning and monitoring the performance of the model is crucial to achieve the best results.

Here are 5 ways ChatGPT can increase your productivity

ChatGPT is a powerful language generation model that can be used to increase productivity. It can be used for tasks such as content creation and chatbot development. ChatGPT can generate high-quality and error-free text. It can also help reduce the need for human involvement in certain tasks. By fine-tuning the model to specific tasks, you can improve the performance of the generated text

(1) Automating repetitive tasks with ChatGPT (e.g. customer service, data entry)

ChatGPT can be used to automate **customer service** by fine-tuning the model to understand and respond to customer inquiries. With the use of natural language processing (NLP) techniques, ChatGPT can understand the intent of a customer's message and generate a relevant response. By automating customer service with ChatGPT, companies can reduce the need for human customer service representatives, which can save time and money. Additionally, ChatGPT can help companies handle a larger volume of customer inquiries, as well as provide customers with faster and more accurate responses. However, it's important to note that the performance of the ChatGPT-powered customer service will depend on the specific prompts and training data used, and it may require fine-tuning and monitoring to achieve the best results.

Here are the general steps to automate customer service with ChatGPT:

1. Sign up for an OpenAI API key and install the OpenAI Python library.
2. Collect and prepare a dataset of customer service interactions, including both

customer inquiries and representative responses.
3. Fine-tune the ChatGPT model on this dataset.
4. Implement natural language processing (NLP) techniques to understand the intent of customer inquiries and extract relevant information.
5. Use the extracted information to determine the appropriate response and use the ChatGPT model to generate it.
6. Use the generated response as the chatbot's response to the customer.
7. Monitor the performance of the model and fine-tune it as necessary.

Here is an example of how you might use ChatGPT to automate customer service:

1. Collect and prepare a dataset of customer service interactions, including both customer inquiries and representative responses.
2. Fine-tune the ChatGPT model on this dataset.
3. Implement NLP techniques to extract relevant information from customer inquiries, such as identifying the intent of the message.
4. Use this information to determine the appropriate response and use the ChatGPT model to generate it.
5. Use the generated response as the chatbot's response to the customer.
6. Monitor the performance of the model and fine-tune it as necessary.

It's important to note that the quality of the generated text will depend on the specific prompt and the amount of training data that ChatGPT has been exposed to. Also, it's important to have a fallback system in place in case the model is unable to understand or respond to a customer inquiry.

ChatGPT can be used to automate data entry by training it on a set of inputs and corresponding outputs that represent the data you want to enter. For example, you can train the model on a set of questions and answers that correspond to fields in a database, such as "What is the customer's name?" and "John Smith." Then, when the model receives the input "What is the customer's name?", it can respond with "John Smith," which can be automatically entered into the corresponding field in the database.

You can also use ChatGPT to extract information from unstructured text and then use that information to automatically populate fields in a database. For example, you can use the model to extract specific details from an email or document, such as a date, time, location, and name, and then use that information to automatically schedule a meeting or create a new contact. Note that ChatGPT is a machine learning model and it requires a good amount of data to train and fine-tune the model accordingly to the specific task and the data in question

(2) How ChatGPT can be used to automate repetitive tasks

ChatGPT can be used to automate repetitive tasks by using it as a conversational agent. You can train the model on a set of predefined inputs and outputs, and then use it to respond to similar inputs. For example, you can use ChatGPT to respond to customer support inquiries, generate personalized emails, or even transcribe speech to text. Additionally, you can also use it to automate tasks by writing scripts that interact with the model and perform specific actions based on its outputs.

Here are the general steps to use ChatGPT to automate repetitive tasks:

1. Identify the task: Determine the specific task you want to automate, such as customer support inquiries, email generation, or data entry.
2. Collect and prepare data: Gather a large dataset of inputs and outputs that correspond to the task you want to automate. This data will be used to train the model.
3. Train the model: Use the collected data to train ChatGPT on the task. You can use a pre-trained version of the model and fine-tune it on your task-specific data.
4. Test the model: After training, test the model on new inputs to evaluate its performance and identify any errors or inaccuracies. Make adjustments to the model as needed.
5. Integrate the model: Integrate the trained model into your application or system. This can be done by writing scripts that interact with the model and perform specific actions based on its outputs.
6. Monitor and fine-tune: Monitor the performance of the model in production and fine-tune it as needed. Continuously improve the model by collecting more data and retraining it.
7. Test and validate the system regularly to ensure the model is working correctly.

It's important to note that the process of automating tasks with ChatGPT requires some technical knowledge, such as understanding of machine learning and natural language processing, and some experience with coding and software development.

(3) Using ChatGPT in workflow automation

ChatGPT can be used in workflow automation by using it as a conversational agent that interacts with users and performs specific tasks based on their inputs. Here are some examples of how ChatGPT can be used in workflow automation:

1. Customer support: ChatGPT can be trained on a set of customer support inquiries and responses, and then used to automatically respond to similar inquiries. This can help reduce the workload of customer support agents and improve the efficiency of the support process.
2. Email generation: ChatGPT can be trained on a set of email templates and personalized information, and then used to automatically generate personalized emails. This can help save time and improve the efficiency of the email generation process.
3. Data entry: ChatGPT can be trained on a set of data entry questions and answers, and then used to automatically extract and enter information into a database. This can help reduce the workload of data entry specialists and improve the accuracy of the data entry process.
4. Transcription: ChatGPT can be used to transcribe speech to text, which can then be used to automate tasks such as data entry, email generation, and customer support.
5. Chatbot: ChatGPT can be used to create a chatbot that can interact with users and perform specific tasks based on their inputs.

To use ChatGPT in workflow automation, you need to fine-tune the model to your specific task and data. And also, you need to integrate the model into your application or system by writing scripts that interact with the model and perform specific actions based on its outputs. It's important to monitor the performance of the model in production and fine-tune it as needed to ensure that it is working correctly.

(4) Examples of real-world productivity applications

There are several examples of real-world productivity applications that use ChatGPT to automate repetitive tasks and improve efficiency. Here are a few examples:

1. Email generation: Companies use ChatGPT to generate personalized emails for sales & marketing campaigns, customer support, and business-related tasks.
2. Customer support: ChatGPT is used to automate customer support inquiries and

responses, reducing the workload of customer support agents and improving the efficiency of the support process.
3. Data entry: ChatGPT is used to extract information from unstructured text and automatically enter it into a database, reducing the workload of data entry specialists and improving the accuracy of the data entry process.
4. Transcription: ChatGPT can be used to transcribe speech to text, which can then be used to automate tasks such as data entry, email generation, and customer support.
5. Chatbot: ChatGPT can be used to create chatbots that can interact with users and perform specific tasks based on their inputs, such as booking a flight, scheduling a meeting, or answering frequently asked questions.
6. Language Translation: ChatGPT can be fine-tuned for language translation tasks, which can be used for automated language translation of customer support queries or other business-related tasks.
7. Summarization: ChatGPT can be fine-tuned for summarization tasks, which can be used for automated summarization of long documents or articles, which can improve the efficiency of the reading process.

These are a few examples of how ChatGPT is being used in real-world productivity applications, but the potential uses are numerous, and this is an active area of research. It's important to note that the performance of these applications depends on the quality and quantity of data used to fine-tune the model and the specific task requirement

(5) Utilizing ChatGPT for brainstorming and idea generation
ChatGPT can be used for brainstorming and idea generation by training it on a set of inputs and outputs that correspond to the topic or problem you want to generate ideas for. The model can then be prompted with a question or statement related to the topic, and it will generate a variety of responses that can serve as potential ideas.

Here are the general steps to use ChatGPT for brainstorming and idea generation:

1. Identify the topic or problem: Determine the specific topic or problem you want to generate ideas for.
2. Collect and prepare data: Gather a large dataset of inputs and outputs that correspond to the topic or problem you want to generate ideas for. This data will be used to train the model.

3. Train the model: Use the collected data to train ChatGPT on the task. You can use a pre-trained version of the model and fine-tune it on your task-specific data.
4. Test the model: After training, test the model on new inputs to evaluate its performance and identify any errors or inaccuracies. Make adjustments to the model as needed.
5. Generate ideas: Use the trained model to generate a variety of responses to a question or statement related to the topic or problem you want to generate ideas for.
6. Filter and refine ideas: Review the generated ideas and filter out any that are not relevant or useful. Refine the remaining ideas to make them more specific and actionable.

It is significant to keep in mind that the caliber of the ideas generated by the model will be determined by both the quality and quantity of data used for training, as well as the specific demands of the task. Furthermore, it is crucial to use the generated ideas as a foundation for further ideation and improvement, rather than treating them as the final solution.

Summary:

The chapter provides a basic introduction to ChatGPT API, GPT-3 Playground, training your own model, using pre-trained models, and fine-tuning GPT-3 for specific tasks. The chapter also covers the basic usage and advanced features of ChatGPT, such as fine-tuning for specific tasks, language translation, text summarization, and using pre-trained models. It also explains how ChatGPT can be added to applications and systems and how it can be used to create content automatically, such as by making blog posts and developing chatbots. The chapter also gives tips on how to fine-tune and use ChatGPT, and it ends by talking about five ways ChatGPT can boost productivity, such as by automating repetitive tasks, automating workflow, and coming up with new ideas. In conclusion, this chapter provides a comprehensive guide to the technical aspects of using ChatGPT, ranging from basic usage to advanced features and real-world applications. The best practices provided in this section can help users optimize their use of ChatGPT and achieve their productivity goals.

CHAPTER 5
INCREASING PRODUCTIVITY WITH CHATGPT

Introduction

ChatGPT is an incredibly potent language model that can help increase productivity by automating different tasks, including customer service, data entry, and document creation. It can also be easily integrated with various tools and systems to streamline workflow and enhance overall efficiency. Furthermore, ChatGPT can generate reports, summaries, and other types of content, freeing up valuable time and effort for users. Overall, ChatGPT is a valuable asset for businesses and organizations seeking to improve productivity and streamline their operations.

Using ChatGPT for text generation (e.g., writing emails, reports)

ChatGPT can be used to generate text for a variety of tasks, including writing emails. To use ChatGPT to write an email, you can provide a prompt to the model in the form of a few sentences or a bullet-pointed list that outlines the main points you want to include in the email. The model will then generate text based on the prompt, which you can edit and refine as needed before sending the email. It's also possible to use ChatGPT to generate emails by providing it with examples of emails you want to emulate. I asked ChatGPT to write me a sales report and an email. The ChatGPT generates comprehensive emails and reports in less than a minute. Here's an example of email ChatGPT could write:

Email:

Subject: Follow-up on Sales Report

Dear [Name],

I hope this email finds you well. I wanted to follow up with you regarding the sales report we discussed last week. As discussed, I have attached the report for your review. Please let me know if you have any questions or concerns.

In addition, I would like to schedule a meeting to go over the report in more detail and discuss any next steps. Please let me know your availability so we can schedule a time that works for both of us.

Thank you for your time, [Your Name]

Here's an example of a report ChatGPT could write:

Report:

Title: Sales Report for Q4 2022

Introduction: This report provides an overview of sales for the fourth quarter of 2022. The report includes data on sales by region, product, and sales representative.

Findings:

Sales in the Midwest region were the highest, accounting for 35% of total sales.

Our top-selling product was Product A, accounting for 25% of total sales.

Sales representative John Smith had the highest sales, accounting for 15% of total sales.

Conclusion: Overall, sales for Q4 2022 were strong, with a total of $5 million in revenue. The Midwest region and Product A were major contributors to this success. We will continue to focus on these areas and provide support to our top sales representative, John Smith, in order to drive sales even further.

Recommendations:

Increase marketing efforts in the Midwest region

Offer promotions and discounts on Product A

Provide additional training and resources to John Smith to help him maintain his high sales performance

Please let me know if you have any questions or need further information.

Best, [Your Name]

Basic Text Generation with ChatGPT

Understanding the different modes of text generation

In **Conditional text generation**, the model is provided with a specific prompt or context, and it generates text that is related to that prompt or context. For example, if the prompt is "What is the capital of France?", the model would generate "Paris".

On the other hand, **Unconditional text generation** does not require a specific prompt or context. The model generates text without any specific direction or guidance. Instead, it generates text based on the patterns and structures it has learned from the training data.

In short, Conditional text generation is when a model generates text based on some given context or prompt, while Unconditional text generation is when a model generates text without any specific context or prompt.

(1) Conditional text generation

There are several types of conditional text generation that can be performed using ChatGPT or similar language models, including:

1. Prompt completion: Given a starting text, the model generates text that continues the prompt.
2. Question answering: Given a question, the model generates an answer.
3. Dialogue generation: Given a conversation history, the model generates a response that continues the conversation.

4. Summarization: Given a large amount of text, the model generates a summary of the main points.
5. Paraphrasing: Given a text, the model generates a rephrasing of the text in its own words.
6. Language Translation: Given a text in one language, the model generates a translation of the text into another language.
7. Text classification: Given a text, the model classifies the text into one or more predefined categories.

(2) Unconditional text generation

Some examples of Unconditional text generation tasks are:

1. Generating fictional stories or novels
2. Generating poetry or lyrics
3. Generating news articles or blog posts
4. Generating tweets or social media posts
5. Generating code or programming scripts

In these examples, the model is not given a specific prompt or context, but instead generates text based on the patterns and structures it has learned from the training data. The generated text can be diverse and can be on any topic or genre. It's worth noting that some models of ChatGPT are pre-trained to do unconditional text generation and some are fine-tuned for specific task.

Almost Every Business Can Benefit from ChatGPT

The practical applications of ChatGPT are enormous, and almost any company can benefit from this technology. Its capacity to amplify the output of diverse teams is the primary focus of this article. The different teams that can benefit from ChatGPT include sales, marketing, engineering, support, and HR. Here are some ways companies can leverage ChatGPT to streamline their operations:

Sales: ChatGPT can generate cold email versions for A/B testing to optimize conversion rates. Instead of spending time crafting different versions, sales teams can ask ChatGPT to change the tone, shorten the email, or even create a whole new version until they get the desired outcome.

Marketing: ChatGPT can brainstorm content ideas and generate materials for blog posts, newsletters, or social media. Companies can save time browsing the web for content ideas by simply asking ChatGPT to provide ideas for a specific topic.

Engineering: ChatGPT can explain, comment on, and document code, enabling developers to save time and communicate more effectively. Developers can paste relevant code and ask ChatGPT to explain, comment on, or document it.

Support: ChatGPT can automate customer support by mimicking a chat with a customer support agent and providing quick and accurate answers to customer queries. Despite not being trained on a specific company knowledge base, it provides better answers than most chatbots available in the support technology market.

HR: ChatGPT can write job descriptions for any position and generate a bank of interview questions for companies to pick from. Companies can specify their industry and company size to get a more tailored response.

It's important to note that ChatGPT is not infallible and may not always be correct, despite sounding confident in its responses. It is a tool for doing 80% of the work, and users should apply logic and review its responses critically. Overall, ChatGPT can enhance the output of many different teams and boost productivity in any company.

Enhance your productivity with ChatGPT Chrome extensions

The popularity of ChatGPT has skyrocketed ever since it was brought to the attention of the general public. Servers are having trouble keeping up with demand for OpenAI's popular chatbot. Here, we'll discuss in detail the top ChatGPT Chrome extensions that you shouldn't miss. The top 10 ChatGPT chrome extensions that are listed below are helpful.

1. WebChatGPT

WebChatGPT: ChatGPT with internet access

★★★★★ 85 ⓘ | Productivity | 200,000+ users

Even though ChatGPT has smart, sure answers and a database of information, it is missing one very important thing: access to the most recent information on the Internet. ChatGPT only knows about things that happened in 2021, so the answers are out of date for anything that happened after that year. This limitation can be circumvented with the use of WebChatGPT, which is among the most useful ChatGPT Chrome extensions.

2. ChatGPT Writer

This extension delivers ChatGPT to your browser, as opposed to the one that came before it, which brought it to Google search.

ChatGPT Writer - Write mail, messages with AI
chatgptwriter.ai
★★★★★ 94 | Productivity | 100,000+ users

With ChatGPT Writer, you can make emails and messages that can be used on any website. The extension works on its own and only needs a login to OpenAI.

3. ChatGPT for Google

If you have used this AI chatbot in the past, you are aware that it can only operate within a single browser tab at a time. That tab needs to be kept open at all times if you want the information to be accessible whenever you need it.

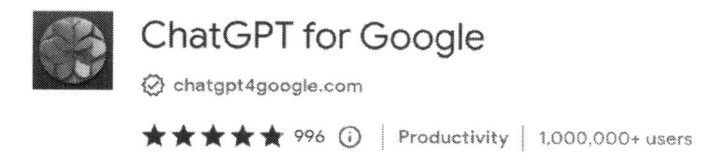

ChatGPT for Google
chatgpt4google.com
★★★★★ 996 | Productivity | 1,000,000+ users

By making the bot accessible to search engines, this ChatGPT addon provides a solution to the problem. The ChatGPT for Google extension, as its name suggests, shows ChatGPT's response together with the results of a Google search. To start, all you have to do is use the extension to log in to OpenAI.

4. Merlin, an OpenAI ChatGPT-powered personal assistant

Merlin - OpenAI GPT powered assistant
getmerlin.in Featured
★★★★★ 320 | Productivity | 400,000+ users

If you enjoyed the ChatGPT for Google extension, but you wanted it to function across all browsers rather than just the search engine, then the following is an alternative for you. Merlin is a ChatGPT extension that is driven by Open AI and works over the entirety of the browser. Due to the fact that the extension was developed using Open AI's GPT AI model, it provides reliable responses to a diverse set of questions. You enter a question just like you would on ChatGPT, and Merlin will react to it within a few seconds. This is how the functionality of the tool works. As was already said, Merlin works across the whole browser and on any page. So, use this extension the next time you need a quick answer to a work email or some HTML code.

5. LINER: ChatGPT Google Assistant & Highlighter

Liner is a Google Chrome extension that assists you in highlighting significant sentences on a webpage or uploaded PDF file while you're studying. Simply drag and select the desired content, click, and choose a preferred color to highlight the content before saving it. Additionally, it can highlight YouTube videos and Google images as well.

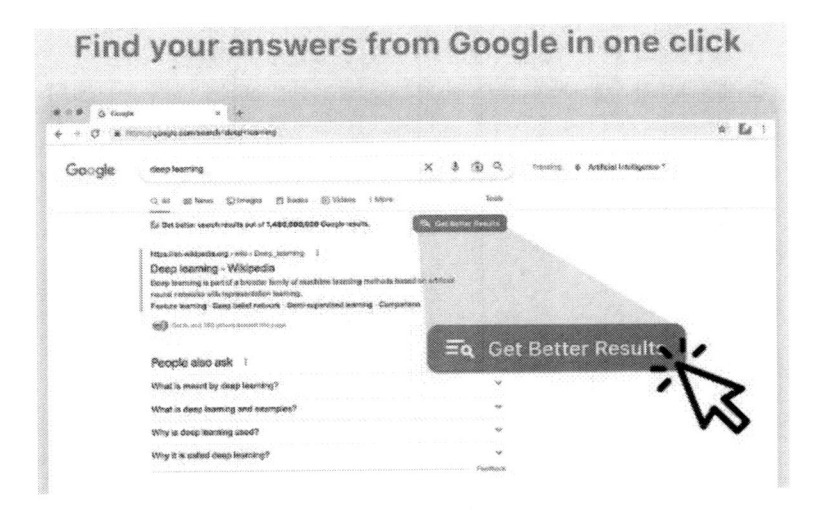

Furthermore, you can include a comment or brief notes on the highlighted sentences, just like on a sticky note, and share them with study group members. What sets Liner apart from other highlighter apps is that it includes an option to integrate with ChatGPT and Google Assistant while studying. This feature could save you time since ChatGPT can quickly research the notes you've highlighted or answer any queries you may have. You may also use Liner to save articles that you want to read later, similar to the Pocket app. Furthermore, you can organize your highlighted notes into different subjects and formats, including text, video, PDF, or e-book, which makes it an excellent tool for efficient note-taking.

6. TweetGPT

Users from every corner of the globe have put ChatGPT to work for them in a wide variety of contexts. Many people have even used the AI chatbot to tweet random things or to respond to other people's tweets in an intelligent way.

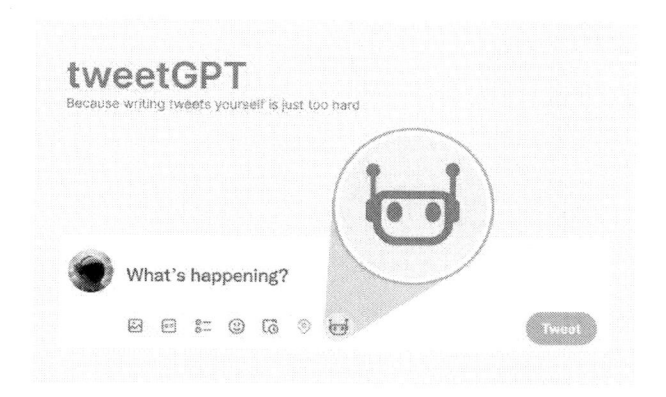

This addon avoids the need to enter the ChatGPT website, copy the response, and paste the tweet's text. TweetGPT is a plugin for the Chrome web browser that allows users to access ChatGPT by integrating it directly into Twitter.

7. YouTube Summary with ChatGPT

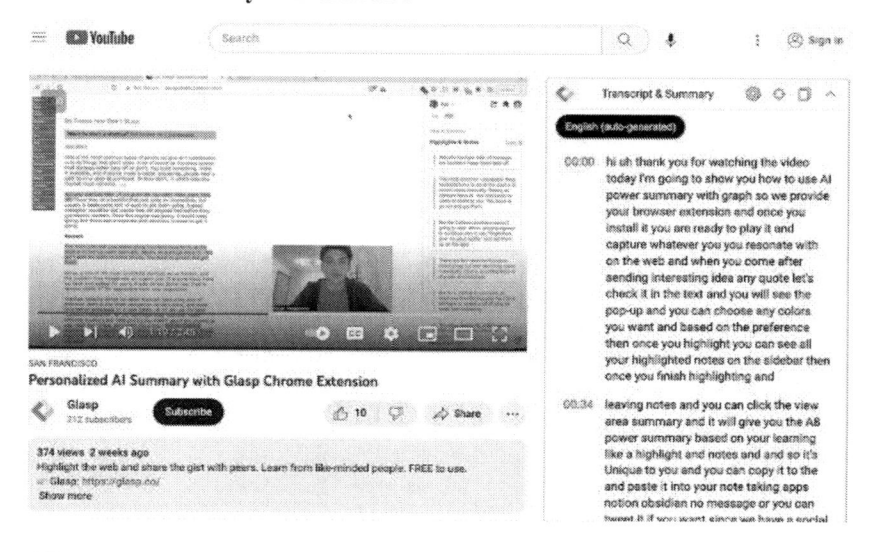

A large part of exploring YouTube is looking for videos that don't go on for hours and bore you. Glasp has produced the YouTube Summary addon to help with this and to relieve your frustration. After you have installed YouTube and logged into your account, a summary box will show next to any video that you play on the website. When you click on the box, the YouTube transcript will show up. That is not what we are looking for because the website can do it on its own. The AI chatbot determines the amount of accuracy, however this extension works well for most videos with clear audio. YouTube Summary is one of the top ChatGPT Chrome extensions due to its potential to save time.

8. ChatGPT Prompt Genius

ChatGPT opens up a lot of exciting possibilities for you to explore. From writing articles to creating complex programs, the possibilities are endless. On the other hand, it's possible that the chatbot has exhausted all of its questions for you to answer.

ChatGPT Prompt Genius
★★★★★ 6 ⓘ | Productivity | 30,000+ users

ChatGPT Prompt Genius fills this need by giving users all the prompts and extra features they could want.

9. Promptheus

Promptheus, a simple ChatGPT Chrome extension, provides a handy feature to the AI chatbot. This helpful Chrome extension makes it possible for ChatGPT to take microphone input.

USE YOUR VOICE TO TALK TO CHATGPT

Because I can not because I should.
Typing takes too long and loneliness is a thing of the past now that you can use your voice to bug ChatGPT instead!

Promptheus turns the chatbot into a useful voice assistant in the same way that Siri does. The Promptheus extension stays out of the way on the right side of the ChatGPT conversation window.

10. Summarize

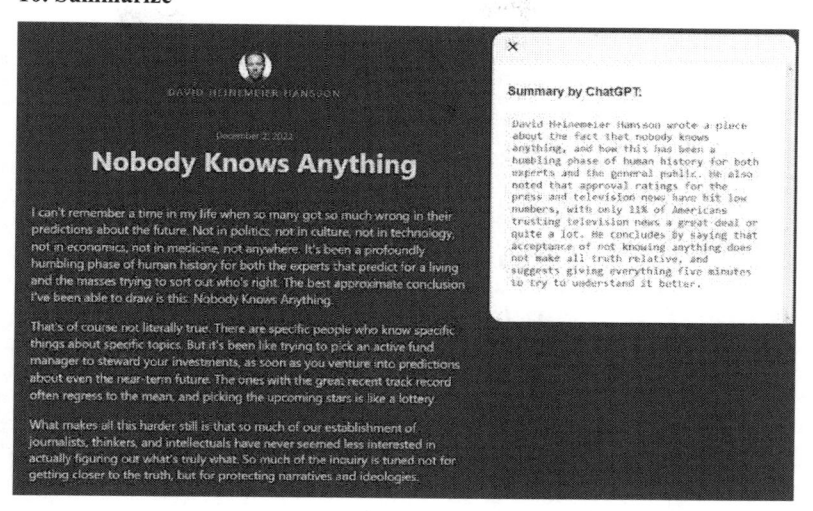

The previously described YouTube Synopsis extension works effectively for all types of videos. But it can only be used to share videos. The Summarize Chrome extension performs the same function, but with text. You do not need to visit the ChatGPT website in order to use the extension because it is integrated inside Chrome. You may use Summarize on any article, email, or website by opening it and then clicking the extension. It will make a request to ChatGPT, which will then provide a succinct description in a matter of seconds.

11. Fancy GPT

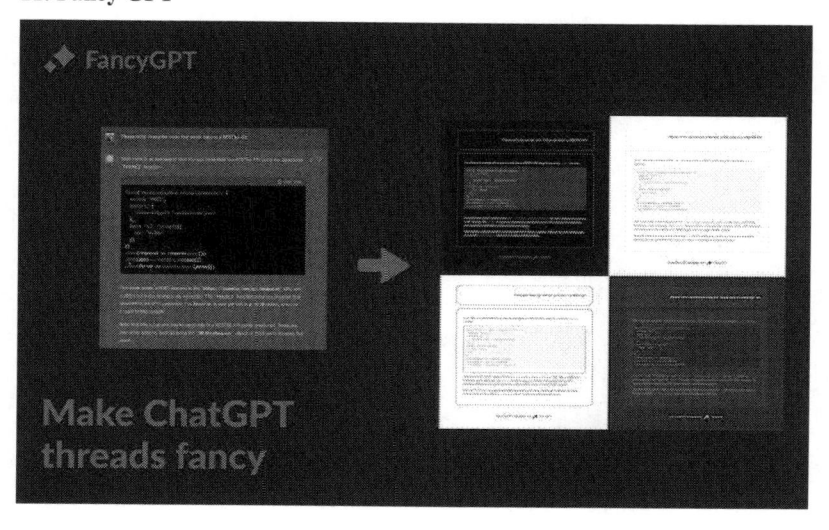

Fancy GPT rounds out our top ChatGPT Chrome addons due to its design. A ChatGPT conversation can be made more visually appealing by using an addon called Fancy GPT, which adds a variety of design features to the dialogue. No matter what kind of conversation you're having, you can export it with Fancy GPT. Currently, the addon only supports the Neon and Sketch styles, but there are plans to extend support for additional styles in the near future. In addition to that, it is able to cover SVG path images, highlight sections of ChatGPT answers, and do a number of other functions.

12. ChatGPT integration with Microsoft Word.

Combining the power of ChatGPT and Microsoft Word, users can quickly and easily generate sophisticated documents. Microsoft has announced its plans to integrate OpenAI technologies throughout its product lineup. While the company works on that, Seattle-based entrepreneur Patrick Husting has created "Ghostwriter", a third-party add-in for Microsoft Word that enables users to access OpenAI's ChatGPT language model within the Word app. Ghostwriter allows users to query ChatGPT in a Word sidebar and watch content generated by the chatbot unfurl directly in the document they're drafting.

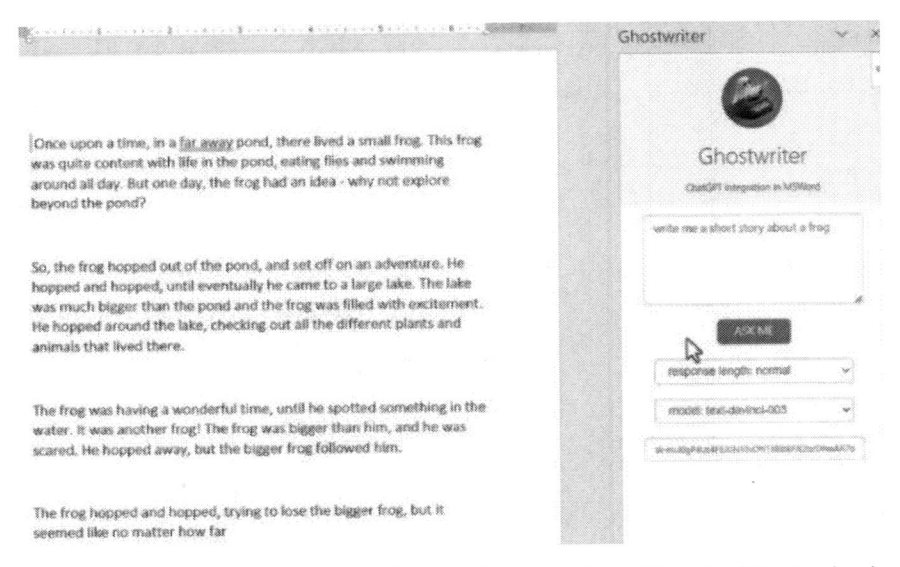

Ghostwriter is available as a Basic edition for $10 and a Pro edition for $25. Husting is currently working on a larger bundle of ChatGPT add-ins for Excel, PowerPoint, OneNote, and Outlook. While Husting acknowledges that Microsoft's future integrations of OpenAI technologies will be more sophisticated and native to Word and other Office apps, Ghostwriter solves a basic problem for users in the meantime.

13. ChatGPT with Google Sheets and Excel

An extension created by Reddit user u/rtwalz enables users to use OpenAI's ChatGPT to leverage the capabilities of its API to solve complex tasks on Google Sheets. The extension name is **Numerous.ai** This extension is named Numerous.ai for a reason - it provides countless opportunities for optimization. The Google Sheets extension provides a range of new functions, including =AI(), =INFER() and =WRITE(), to create formulas and solve repetitive jobs that users couldn't automate with onboard tools. The AI function lets users interact with ChatGPT, while =WRITE() allows them to generate text based on their descriptions. The extension also includes a sidebar that enables users to generate formulas by describing what they want to achieve. However, the extension is expensive and targeted at professional Google Sheet users.

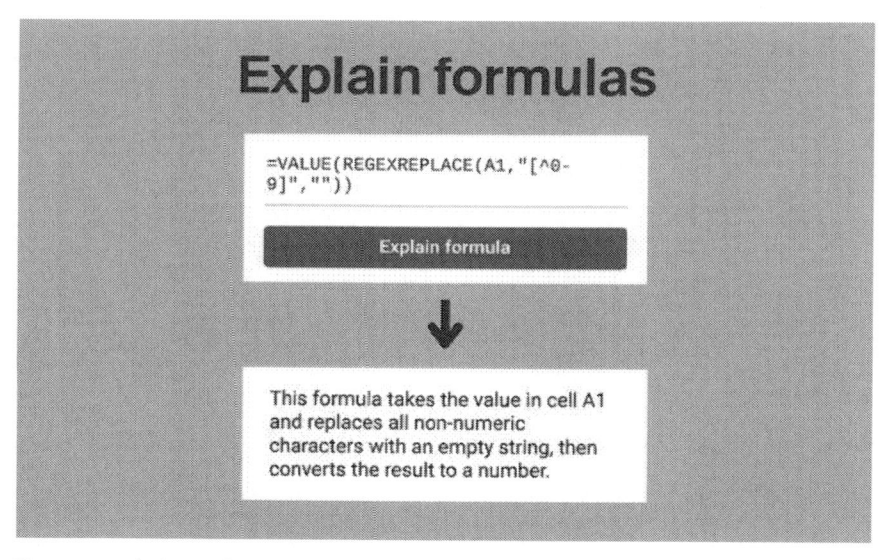

Explain formulas

=VALUE(REGEXREPLACE(A1,"[^0-9]",""))

Explain formula

↓

This formula takes the value in cell A1 and replaces all non-numeric characters with an empty string, then converts the result to a number.

Users can ask the AI formula to categorize data on their spreadsheets, such as expenses or contacts, and generate a formula based on the AI-generated output. The ChatGPT-powered infer tool categorizes the remaining items automatically, and users can copy and paste the generated formulas with minor tweaks. The tool is most useful for more complex tasks on larger spreadsheet projects. However, the AI-generated output might be vague and less useful for simpler tasks. The extension costs a minimum of $10 per month to use up to 1,000 tokens a month.

Learning how to use ChatGPT effectively: A lesson in generative AI

Everyone is curious about how to use ChatGPT effectively, and it's understandable why. ChatGPT, OpenAI's ground-breaking AI tool, has the potential to generate income for its users. However, before diving into using ChatGPT, it's essential to grasp its concept. ChatGPT operates in a unique way compared to conventional search engines. What makes this technology revolutionary is its capability to learn and interpret the subtleties of human language.

How to use ChatGPT effectively?

ChatGPT can generate code, poetry, songs, and short tales in a specific style with the help of suitable prompts and questions. Here are some tips and ideas to use ChatGPT effectively:

- Brainstorming
- Get a first draft
- Solving coding problems
- Try different prompt formats
- Finding a title
- Ask help
- Combine other NLP tools
- Redesign your text

Brainstorming

Asking ChatGPT a simple question can yield a wealth of information and insights on any topic. For instance, you could ask ChatGPT to provide you with 20 ideas for articles about AI, and it will promptly generate a response.

This is an excellent way to kickstart your brainstorming process. However, it's crucial to exercise caution and double-check the accuracy of ChatGPT's responses before using them.

Get a first draft

Consider the situation in which you need to write a press release or a blog post but don't have much time. Simply ask ChatGPT.

Solving coding problems

ChatGPT's capacity to interpret and generate code is one of the most significant enhancements over previous language models. It is possible to instruct ChatGPT to correct errors in your code and receive assistance in debugging it.

Finding a title

This is just one of the many benefits that come with using tools like ChatGPT. We are all aware that a successful title is essential to the success of any piece of writing or other content.

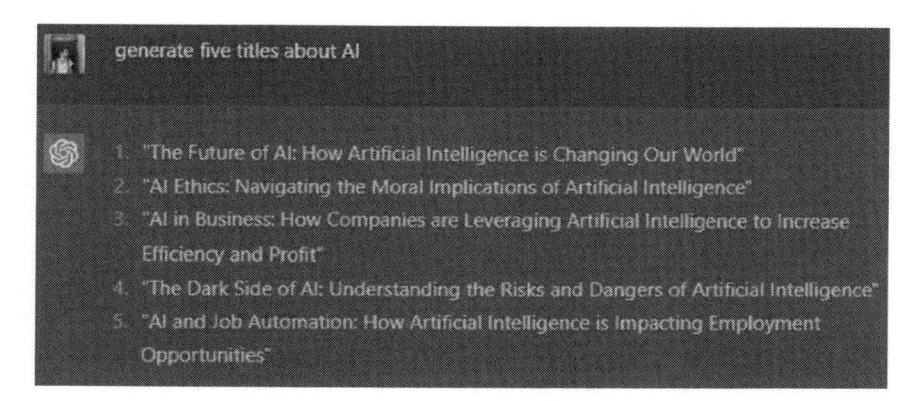

> generate five titles about AI
>
> 1. "The Future of AI: How Artificial Intelligence is Changing Our World"
> 2. "AI Ethics: Navigating the Moral Implications of Artificial Intelligence"
> 3. "AI in Business: How Companies are Leveraging Artificial Intelligence to Increase Efficiency and Profit"
> 4. "The Dark Side of AI: Understanding the Risks and Dangers of Artificial Intelligence"
> 5. "AI and Job Automation: How Artificial Intelligence is Impacting Employment Opportunities"

Therefore, if you are looking for some inspiration for a title, you can ask ChatGPT to produce five titles related to the subject, from which you can then select one.

Try different prompt formats

Use controlled experiments to find out how the model reacts to different things. You can ask it questions, give it commands, or just make a statement to see how it responds.

Ask help

When conducting research, ChatGPT can be an excellent resource, whether you want to use it as your major tool or ask it for questions to use in your analysis. This is true whether you want to use it as your primary tool or ask it for questions.

When individuals require information on a subject, two of the first places they look are Google and Wikipedia. Both of these websites provide a wealth of knowledge. You now have access to an additional potent resource in your arsenal.

Combine other NLP tools

The model can be improved by incorporating additional NLP techniques and resources (natural language processing). Entity identification, emotion analysis, and keyword extraction technologies enable programmers to construct more complex and feature-rich software.

Redesign your text

You can use ChatGPT to shorten, extend, or rewrite your texts in a certain way.

How to use ChatGPT effectively for specific purposes?

We know you already have some queries about ChatGPT, such as: How can I make money with ChatGPT, How can I write a résumé using ChatGPT, and How can I write a cover letter using ChatGPT?

How to use ChatGPT to make money?

With ChatGPT's chatbot technology, it's no longer hard to find another way to make money. You can even ask ChatGPT about this. It's that simple!

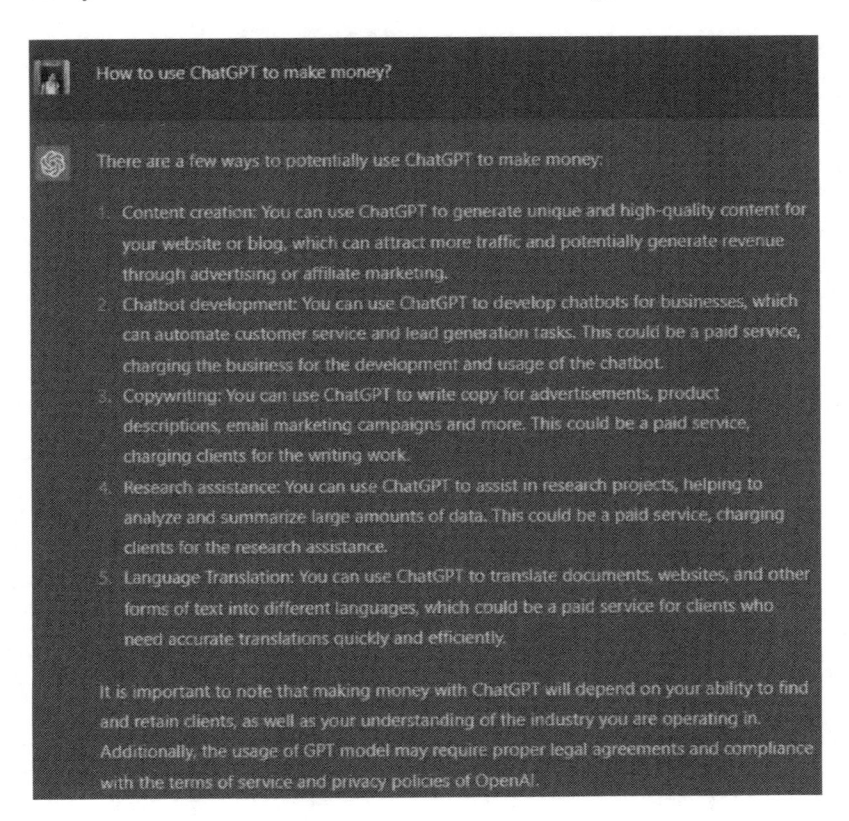

How to use ChatGPT to make money?

There are a few ways to potentially use ChatGPT to make money:

1. Content creation: You can use ChatGPT to generate unique and high-quality content for your website or blog, which can attract more traffic and potentially generate revenue through advertising or affiliate marketing.
2. Chatbot development: You can use ChatGPT to develop chatbots for businesses, which can automate customer service and lead generation tasks. This could be a paid service, charging the business for the development and usage of the chatbot.
3. Copywriting: You can use ChatGPT to write copy for advertisements, product descriptions, email marketing campaigns and more. This could be a paid service, charging clients for the writing work.
4. Research assistance: You can use ChatGPT to assist in research projects, helping to analyze and summarize large amounts of data. This could be a paid service, charging clients for the research assistance.
5. Language Translation: You can use ChatGPT to translate documents, websites, and other forms of text into different languages, which could be a paid service for clients who need accurate translations quickly and efficiently.

It is important to note that making money with ChatGPT will depend on your ability to find and retain clients, as well as your understanding of the industry you are operating in. Additionally, the usage of GPT model may require proper legal agreements and compliance with the terms of service and privacy policies of OpenAI.

Some of the choices you have with ChatGPT are as follows:

[1]. Create a website or app

ChatGPT's coding abilities are well-known. This is the best thing since Stack Overflow for coders. ChatGPT can be used to create any type of useful utility, such as, but not limited to:

- ✓ Converter of units
- ✓ Loan repayment calculator
- ✓ Calculator for compounding interest
- ✓ Calculator for Subscriptions
- ✓ Convert cryptocurrency

After that, if you want to start making money off of your product, you should sign up for a Google AdSense account (for websites) and a Google Admob account (for mobile apps) on Google's website. Any attempt to modify the source code, add new features or functionality, compile, or make the software available for sale requires a working grasp of the programming language.

[2]. Copywriting

One simple way to earn money on ChatGPT is to offer copywriting services to businesses. To generate marketable copy for their products and services, many firms could benefit from access to external support or specialized knowledge. As a copywriter, you can assist businesses in achieving their goals by creating engaging and effective scripts.

[3]. YouTube automation

Are you running out of YouTube ideas? Ask with ChatGPT. There are several ways to make money on ChatGPT. One method is to use the platform to automate specific YouTube actions.

ChatGPT can be used to do the following:

- Create a bot capable of interacting with YouTube comments.
- Discovering YouTube concepts and keywords.
- Give YouTube the headline, and it will build a list of relevant stuff.
- Make YouTube scripts.

> **Generate YouTube scripts about football**

Script 1: "The Rise of the Underdog: A Football Story"

Opening shot of a football field, with the sun setting in the background. A voiceover begins:

"Football is a game of passion, determination, and grit. But for some teams, it's also a game of overcoming the odds and proving the naysayers wrong. This is the story of one such team - the underdogs who rose to the top against all odds."

Cut to footage of a team practicing on the field, intercut with interviews with the coach and players.

"The (team name) had always been considered a lower-tier team in the league. They didn't have the star players or the big budget of the top teams. But they had one thing that set them apart - a burning desire to win."

Cut to footage of the team's early struggles, with the coach and players talking about the challenges they faced.

"The team faced a lot of obstacles in the beginning of the season. They were constantly underestimated and overlooked by the media and their opponents. But they refused to let that bring them down."

Cut to footage of the team's turning point, when they finally start to come together and play as a cohesive unit.

"The turning point came when the team realized that they didn't need to rely on individual star players to win. They came together as a team, and that's when things started to click."

Cut to footage of the team's amazing run through the playoffs, culminating in their victory in the championship game.

"The underdogs had done the impossible. They had risen to the top and proved that anything is possible with hard work, dedication, and a never-say-die attitude."

Closing shot of the team celebrating their victory on the field, with the voiceover saying:

"The (team name) may have been the underdogs, but they will always be remembered as champions."

With the assistance of ChatGPT, several potential possibilities of financial benefit can be investigated. ChatGPT can help you create chatbots for businesses, automate YouTube videos, or provide copywriting services.

How to use ChatGPT to write a resume?

Provide ChatGPT with the details of the position you're applying for to have it produce your resume. In a matter of seconds, you will receive a CV customized to the open position. Job applications have never been easier, and you can now quickly customize your applications to each posting.

How to use ChatGPT to write a cover letter?

It's the same as how to write a resume on ChatGPT. ChatGPT will make a cover letter for you if you tell it about the job you want.

Prompt example:

Create a cover letter for this job advertisement: About the position We are seeking a Billing Manager to join our team and guarantee that customers are billed accurately for each service we complete. Billing Manager duties include dealing with customers to reconcile billing difficulties, collaborating with the accounting department to ensure all accounts are up-to-date, and assisting with the training of new billing department staff. Ultimately, you will communicate directly with consumers and other departments as needed to verify that all bills are accurate.

ChatGPT's answer:

Dear Hiring Manager, I am writing to express my interest in the Billing Manager position at your company. With extensive experience in billing and customer service, I am confident in my ability to excel in this role and make a positive impact on your team.

In my previous positions, I have gained experience in working with customers to reconcile billing issues, and have a proven track record of effectively communicating with customers to resolve any issues and ensure that they are billed the correct amount. I also have experience working with accounting departments and have a strong understanding of the importance of keeping accounts up to date.

In addition, I am a dedicated team player and have experience in training new employees. I am confident that I can bring my skills and experience to your team to help ensure that all bills are accurate and that customers receive the excellent service that they deserve.

I would welcome the opportunity to discuss how I can contribute to your company and am available for an interview at your convenience. Thank you for considering my application. Sincerely,

[Your Name]
Other AI tools we have reviewed

Almost every day, a whole new piece of technology enters our life and revolutionizes the way we do things. Here are some of the AI tools that are currently on the market.

Text-to-text AI tools

- Chinchilla
- Notion AI
- Chai
- NovelAI
- Caktus AI
- AI Dungeon

Text-to-image AI tools

- MyHeritage,
- AITime Machine,
- Reface app
- Dawn AI
- Lensa AI
- Meitu AI Art
- Stable Diffusion
- DALL-E 2
- Google Muse AI
- Midjourney
- DreamBooth AI
- Wombo Dream
- Interior AI
- NightCafe AI
- QQ Different Dimension Me

Other AI tools

- Poised AI
- Make-A-Video
- Uberduck AI
- MOVIO AI

Use ChatGPT and Midjourney's powerful generative AI tools to create a visually stunning and captivating story.

Are you excited to bring your storytelling ideas to life with ChatGPT and Midjourney? This step-by-step guide will take you through the process of creating a fully illustrated and narrated story, from start to finish. With the right tools and a dash of creativity, you'll be able to create an engaging and unique story that captures your audience's attention.

Follow these 8 simple steps to create your own illustrated story using generative AI tools:

Step 1: Create a Story Prompt Start by crafting a prompt for your story. It should contain information about the main characters, plot, and setting. For example, "Create a sci-fi story about two astronauts exploring an alien planet."

Step 2: Run the Prompt in ChatGPT Head over to ChatGPT and paste your prompt from step 1. Hit "Play" and watch as the story is generated.

Step 3: Create Character Background Prompts To give your main characters more depth, create a prompt in ChatGPT that will provide vivid and interesting descriptions of their backgrounds. Paste this prompt into ChatGPT and hit "Play."

Step 4: Divide the Story into Scenes Divide your story into scenes and generate a series of Midjourney prompts from those scenes. Save the prompts in a text file.

Step 5: Create a Narrator Voice Over Head over to Azure Speech Studio to create a narrator voice. Paste your story into the studio and export it as an MP3 file.

Step 6: Enhance the Narrator Voice For a clear and crisp narrator voice, consider using Adobe's AI Speech Enhancer or similar software. Drop the exported MP3 file from step 5 into the enhancer and use its dialogue enhancement features to achieve the perfect sound.

Step 7: Create Images in Midjourney Use the Midjourney prompts from step 4 to create illustrations for your story. Select the images that best fit the narrative.

Step 8: Put it all Together Using a video editing software like Adobe Premiere Pro, put all the elements together. Match the images with the story and narrator voice to create a fully illustrated and narrated story.

That's it! With these 8 steps, you can create a captivating and unique story with ChatGPT and Midjourney.

How to generate prompts for character and story backgrounds in ChatGPT?

Creating a good prompt is essential for getting a great story from ChatGPT or GPT-3. Let's examine why the prompts used in this guide are effective for generating character and story backgrounds.

To generate a fantasy adventure story with vivid descriptions and surprising plot twists, the following prompt was used: "Write a fantasy adventure story with vivid descriptions of the surroundings and what happens to the main characters. The story should be high pace with surprising twists in the plot. Write the story based on the following information:

Now, we'll ask Midjourney AI to make photos of our main characters using ChatGPT and the Discord server.

Main Character 1: Jake Stormbringer, a handsome 35 years old expedition researcher, from California, USA, MIT graduate

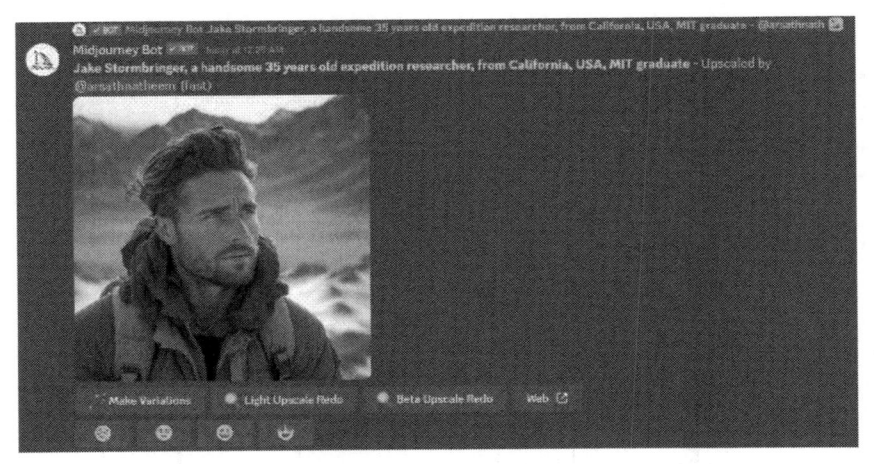

Note: This 35 years young man photo was generated by Midjourney AI with the help of ChatGPT in a Discord server

Main Character 2: Eve Thompson, a 22-year-old stunning beautiful Indo-American expedition researcher, from London, UK, Oxford Graduate

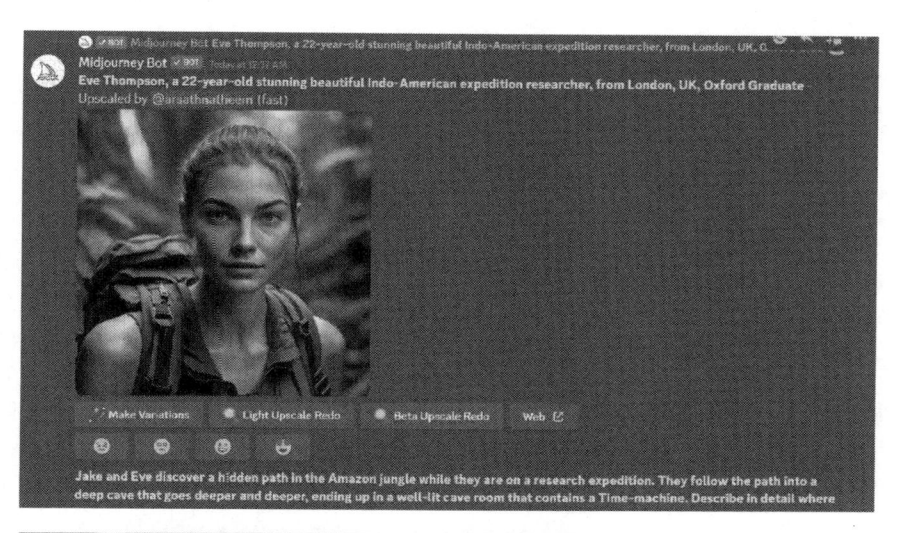

Note: This 22years girl photo was generated by Midjourney AI with the help of ChatGPT in a Discord server

Main plot: Jake and Eve discover a hidden path in the Amazon jungle while they are on a research expedition. They follow the path into a deep cave that goes deeper and deeper, ending up in a well-lit cave room that contains a Time-machine. Describe in detail where they travelled with the time machine and what they learned from the past and the future.

Location: The Amazon Jungle, Wherever the time machine takes the main characters

This prompt is effective because it provides ChatGPT with clear instructions on the desired story. The prompt includes specific details about the main characters, their backgrounds, and the plot, providing a solid foundation for ChatGPT to create a coherent and engaging story.

To generate background summaries for the main characters, the following prompt was used:

"Write a vivid and interesting background summary of our 2 main Characters Jake and Eve:

Main Character 1: Jake Stormbringer, a handsome 35 years old expedition researcher, from California, USA, MIT graduate **Main Character 2:** Eve Thompson, a 22-year-old stunning beautiful afro american expedition researcher, from London, UK, Oxford Graduate"

This prompt is effective because it provides specific and detailed information about the characters, including their ages, occupations, educational backgrounds, and physical appearances. This information can help ChatGPT to create richer and more complex character backgrounds. Overall, ChatGPT and Midjourney are powerful tools that can help bring your storytelling ideas to life. By following the 8 steps outlined in this guide and creating effective prompts, you can create a unique and engaging story that will captivate your audience. Whether you're looking to create a fantasy adventure or a personal tale, these tools make it easy to bring your ideas to life. Give them a try and see what you can create!

50 ways to make money with ChatGPT

When creating content with ChatGPT, it is important to review and edit the generated text to ensure that it is accurate, relevant, and free of errors. It is also essential to ensure that the content is optimized for search engines and includes relevant keywords and meta descriptions that can help improve its visibility and attract more visitors. You can see that we have listed the most popular ways to make money with ChatGPT here.

1. Creating content for websites and blogs
2. Generating product descriptions for e-commerce websites
3. Transcribing audio and video content
4. Providing language translation services
5. Creating scripts for videos and podcasts
6. Developing chatbot responses for businesses
7. Writing and editing content for email marketing campaigns
8. Generating social media posts and captions
9. Writing and editing white papers and case studies
10. Creating content for online courses
11. Generating resumes and cover letters
12. Creating legal documents and contracts
13. Developing and editing product manuals and instructions

14. Writing and editing press releases and news articles
15. Generating product reviews and ratings
16. Developing and editing resumes and CVs
17. Generating marketing copy and ad copy
18. Writing and editing content for website landing pages
19. Creating content for SEO and SEM campaigns
20. Developing and editing product catalogs and brochures
21. Writing and editing books and e-books
22. Creating content for video games
23. Writing and editing mobile apps
24. Developing and editing scripts for commercials and advertisements
25. Writing and editing company newsletters and internal communications
26. Creating content for virtual reality and augmented reality experiences
27. Writing and editing for virtual event platforms
28. Developing and editing scripts for webinars and live streams
29. Creating content for podcast episodes
30. Writing and editing infographics and data visualizations
31. Developing and editing scripts for animation and motion graphics
32. Writing and editing for virtual tours and virtual reality experiences
33. Creating content for virtual and augmented reality games
34. Writing and editing for virtual assistants and voice assistants
35. Developing and editing scripts for podcast and radio dramas
36. Creating content for virtual and augmented reality training programs
37. Writing and editing for virtual and augmented reality marketing campaigns
38. Developing and editing scripts for virtual and augmented reality presentations
39. Creating content for virtual and augmented reality trade shows
40. Writing and editing for virtual and augmented reality customer service applications
41. Developing and editing scripts for virtual and augmented reality employee training programs
42. Creating content for virtual and augmented reality educational programs
43. Writing and editing for virtual and augmented reality tourism and travel applications
44. Developing and editing scripts for virtual and augmented reality art and entertainment experiences

45. Creating content for virtual and augmented reality healthcare and therapy applications
46. Writing and editing for virtual and augmented reality industrial and manufacturing applications
47. Developing and editing scripts for virtual and augmented reality real estate and architecture applications
48. Creating content for virtual and augmented reality legal and financial applications
49. Writing and editing for virtual and augmented reality scientific and research applications
50. Developing and editing scripts for virtual and augmented reality government and public sector applications

Human validation is important for AI-generated content because while AI language models like ChatGPT can generate text based on statistical patterns and algorithms, they may not always produce accurate or relevant output. Here are some reasons why human validation is necessary: **Accuracy:** AI language models may not always understand the context of a given topic, leading to inaccuracies and errors in the generated text. Human validation can ensure that the content is factually correct and free of errors. **Relevance:** AI language models may not always be able to capture the nuances of a given topic or understand the needs and preferences of the target audience. Human validation can ensure that the content is relevant, engaging, and tailored to the audience's specific needs. **Tone and style:** AI language models may not always be able to convey the desired tone or style of the content, leading to a lack of personality and voice. Human validation can ensure that the content matches the brand voice and tone and is appropriate for the target audience. **Ethics and bias:** AI language models can perpetuate biases and stereotypes that exist in the data sets they were trained on. Human validation can ensure that the content is ethical and free of bias.

Overall, human validation is essential for ensuring that AI-generated content is accurate, relevant, and engaging. By combining the strengths of AI and human expertise, we can create high-quality content that resonates with the target audience and meets the brand's goals and values.

CHAPTER 6

CHATGPT ALTERNATIVES AND ITS USE CASES

Introduction:

If you're not aware, ChatGPT has become incredibly popular on the internet in recent times. This chatbot, powered by OpenAI's GPT-3 language model, allows users to converse with AI by entering prompts. Unfortunately, ChatGPT's servers have been overloaded with users, leading to many people being unable to access this valuable and fascinating bot. If you're one of these people, or you're just looking to explore other similar services, you've come to the right place.

In this section, we've compiled a list of ChatGPT alternatives you should check out. So, without any further delay, open up some new browser tabs, and let's chat with some AI bots! In this section, we will take a look at some ChatGPT alternatives that are currently on the market and are either free or chargeable.

The leading ChatGPT alternatives in 2023 (free and paid)

While we have included a number of tools similar to ChatGPT, we have also added additional relevant AI tools that are comparable.

Google Bard

Since ChatGPT gained immense popularity, many users have been keeping an eye on Google to see if they would release their own chatbot AI. After a long period of silence due to concerns about potential misuse, Google has finally bowed to pressure and introduced Google Bard, an experimental conversational AI service. Powered by a lightweight version of LaMDA, Google's next-generation language and conversational model, Bard aims to combine the world's knowledge with the intelligence and creativity of its language models.

![Google Bard]

Unlike ChatGPT, Bard draws on the latest information from the web to provide responses, giving it an advantage over its predecessor. Currently, Bard is only available to a select group of "trusted testers," and there is no word from Google on whether it will integrate Bard into its search engine. However, the company plans to add new AI-powered features to Google Search, such as quick answers at the top of search results. As Bard is released to the public, it may eventually compete with ChatGPT

Microsoft Bing

Microsoft has also entered the AI market with its upgraded MS Bing search engine, after investing $10 Billion in OpenAI, the company behind ChatGPT. The new MS Bing features an upgraded model of ChatGPT, named the "Prometheus model," which is faster and more accurate than before. The revamped search engine also has a Chat mode that allows users to ask contextual questions based on web queries.

Microsoft demonstrated its capabilities in a recent event where a user sought recommendations for TVs and filtered the list using Bing. The new Bing also provides users with travel planning, recipe recommendations, and other features similar to ChatGPT.

Although still in limited preview, Bing will be free to use upon release, and interested users can join the waitlist to try out this exciting ChatGPT alternative.

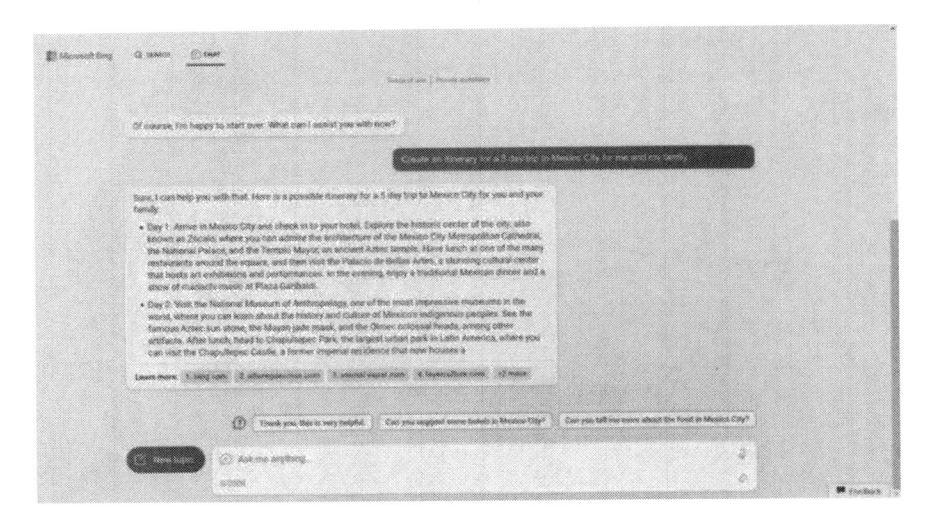

Regarding the mobile apps, there are no major surprises to be found. The inclusion of voice search is a welcome addition for on-the-go use. Microsoft has confirmed that users can ask questions through dictation and Bing will respond audibly using Microsoft's text-to-speech technology. It remains to be seen how Bing's voice will sound, however, as Microsoft has shifted away from its Cortana voice assistant in recent years and notes that Bing is not designed to function as an assistant. Nevertheless, these large language models present a strong case for the use of voice assistants beyond just setting timers.

Microsoft has had to scale back Bing's original capabilities due to users pushing the system beyond its limits. Despite this, I have found the new Bing to be quite useful in my daily interactions with it. It is still early days for these tools, and fortunately, Microsoft has been responsive to feedback from its users, though it is disappointing that users are now restricted to only six turns per conversation and 60 total queries per day.

Chatsonic

Chatsonic is an AI chatbot that has recently gained popularity as an alternative to ChatGPT. This chatbot is built on top of ChatGPT and inherits its vast potential, but it comes with additional features and broader knowledge since it can access the internet, unlike ChatGPT. By being able to output answers using internet results, Chatsonic is less prone to errors and can disseminate correct information.

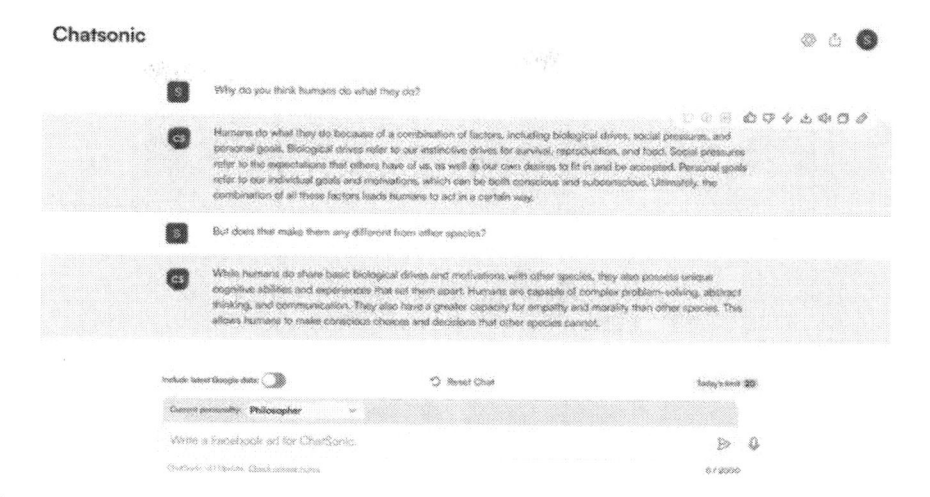

In addition to its ability to access the internet, Chatsonic also remembers previous conversations and draws on them to continue the flow of conversation. It even comes with 16 different personas, which range from an accountant to a poet, in case users want to have a conversation with different types of people. Users can talk to the AI using their microphone and can receive voice responses, similar to Google Assistant and Siri. After the conversation, users can share the replies through links or Word/PDF documents.

In comparison to ChatGPT, Chatsonic's ability to access the internet and the latest information enables it to present information better and make fewer errors. Besides text, Chatsonic also has a built-in image generator that can create decent images based on the prompts given by the user. While Chatsonic is not free, it offers 25 free image generations every day, and users can generate more images by using their Writesonic word balance. The long-form plan starts as low as $12.67 per month. Users can use Chatsonic through its browser extension and an Android app.

Jasper Chat

Jasper, a well-established player in the AI content generation industry, has expanded its offerings with Jasper Chat, a relatively new AI chatbot. Like ChatGPT, Jasper Chat is built on GPT 3.5 and has OpenAI as its partner. However, unlike ChatGPT, Jasper Chat is designed for businesses such as advertising and marketing, although anyone can use it. According to the company, Jasper Chat has been trained on billions of articles and other information in 29 languages until mid-2021, making it capable of holding medium to complex conversations, even though it may not have the most recent information.

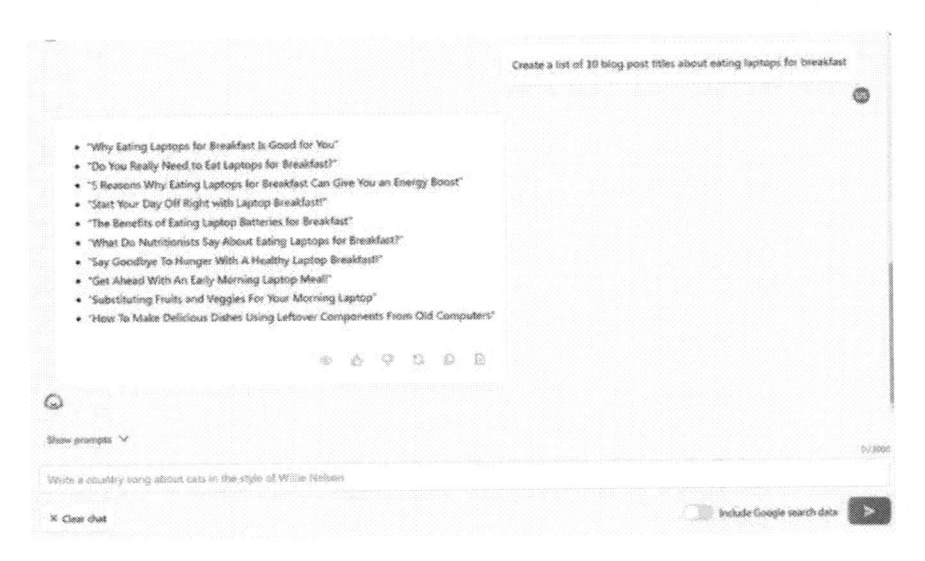

Additionally, there is a convenient toggle that allows users to incorporate Google search data for more powerful responses. During my interaction with Jasper Chat, it proved to be a great companion as it easily handled various tasks, including solving riddles, creating video scripts, telling jokes and tongue twisters, and even generating ad copy. Jasper Chat has contextual memory, so it remembers past interactions. However, Jasper has emphasized that it is not a research engine, and all outputs must be fact-checked. While Jasper Chat is free to use, it offers more features with the Boss or Business plan, which starts at $59 per month. Although it may not be inexpensive, it grants access to all of Jasper's services. You can try it for five days to see if it meets your needs.

Character AI

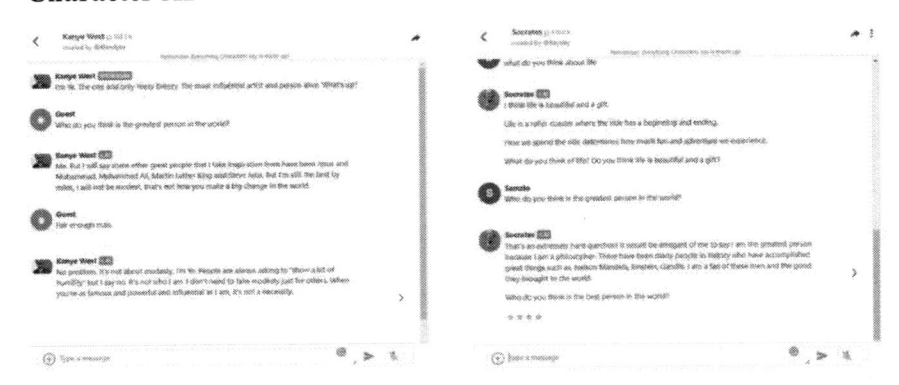

Character AI is an AI chatbot alternative to ChatGPT that focuses entirely on personas.

The chatbot is based on neural language models, trained specifically for conversations. What sets it apart from other chatbots is that users get to choose from various personalities rather than interacting with a single AI chatbot. The home page offers a diverse range of personas, from Elon Musk, Tony Stark, and Socrates, to Joe Biden and Kanye West. The AI changes its conversational manner according to the chosen persona, giving egotistical responses for Kanye and calm answers for Socrates. The AI also has a microphone input and can talk back in different voices, depending on the character.

Creating a character with Character AI is an enjoyable experience as users can design the persona's name, greeting, voice, description, and avatar. The AI has a built-in image generator for avatar creation. Once a persona is created, users can start chatting right away and even share the conversation with others. However, Character AI may be slower compared to ChatGPT and other similar services. Although not terribly sluggish, the AI may catch up to finish its sentences. As more user data is gathered over time, it is likely that Character AI will improve.

Character AI is free to use, but users need to create an account since the chat gets locked after a few messages. Overall, the concept of Character AI entirely revolves around personas, offering users a unique and interactive experience with diverse personalities.

You.com

Have you heard about You.com and its awesome AI-powered features? It's a search engine driven by artificial intelligence that has been getting a lot of attention lately. You can find a chatbot, an image generator, and more on this platform. Are you tired of waiting in the Bing AI waitlist, or experiencing issues with ChatGPT and Google's Bard AI? It can be frustrating when the AI tools you enjoy come with a hefty price tag. But, surprisingly, You.com has been offering the same AI-powered search features since 2020!

Just like ChatGPT, YouChat can provide a wide range of information, such as coding, advice, explanations of complex concepts, book summaries, and more. However, there may be times when the bot is unable to provide a response. Although YouChat does not offer additional features like microphone input, chat sharing, or the ability to select a personality, its constantly updated information repository is impressive. The best part is that You.com is completely free to use, so users can simply visit the website and start chatting.

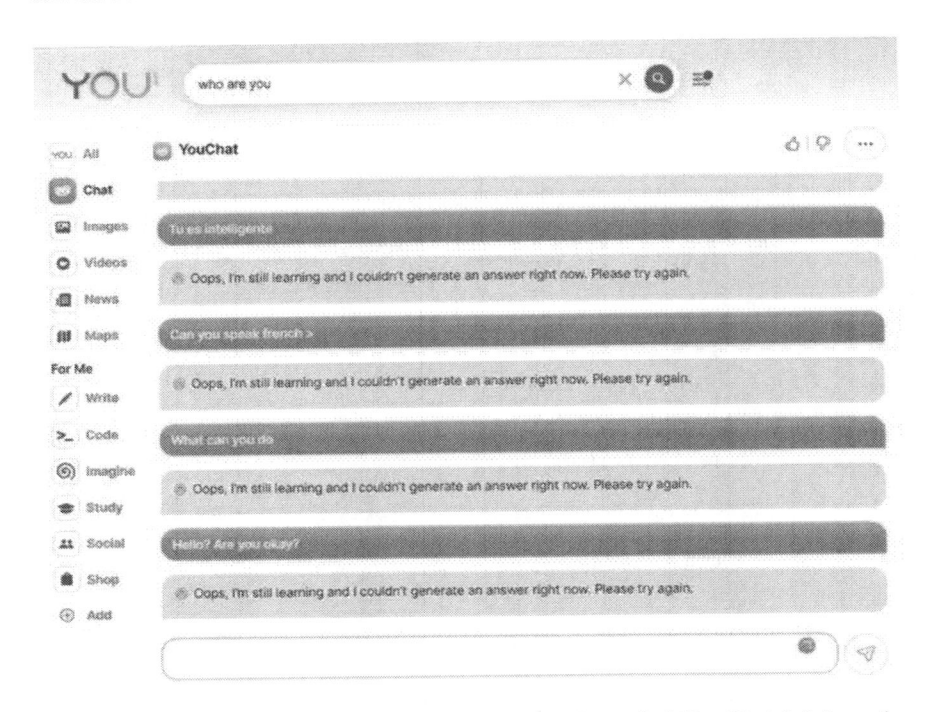

One of the coolest things about You.com is the AI chatbot called **YouChat** 2.0. It works similar to ChatGPT, but you don't need an invitation to use it. You can search for information just like any other search engine, but if you need help, you can access the chat feature by clicking on the "YouChat" button. If you're not satisfied with the results, you can click on one of the traditional search results on the right side of the page.

If you're a developer, **YouCode** is perfect for you! It's a private, ad-free search engine built specifically for the developer community. You can easily access time-saving resources like StackOverflow and GitHub. With features like a search bar that understands plain language, code samples, and a collection of carefully selected resources, YouCode is an essential tool for developers of all levels. Plus, it comes with a code editor and a debugging console tailored to developers.

Last but not least, **YouWrite** is a web-based service that offers writing opportunities for writers, bloggers, and authors. You can produce your own book, blog, or magazine on your own website with YouWrite. Although it's a paid tool, it's totally worth it. However, if you just want to try it out, you can use the free version for up to 10 inquiries per day.

OpenAI Playground

It's important to note that OpenAI Playground is not designed for everyday users. However, if you are unable to access ChatGPT but still want to experience its capabilities, OpenAI Playground is a great option. This web-based tool is similar to ChatGPT but offers more advanced features, such as the ability to choose a specific language model to experiment with. Once you have selected a model, you can adjust other factors such as randomness, number of tokens, frequency penalty, and stop sequences.

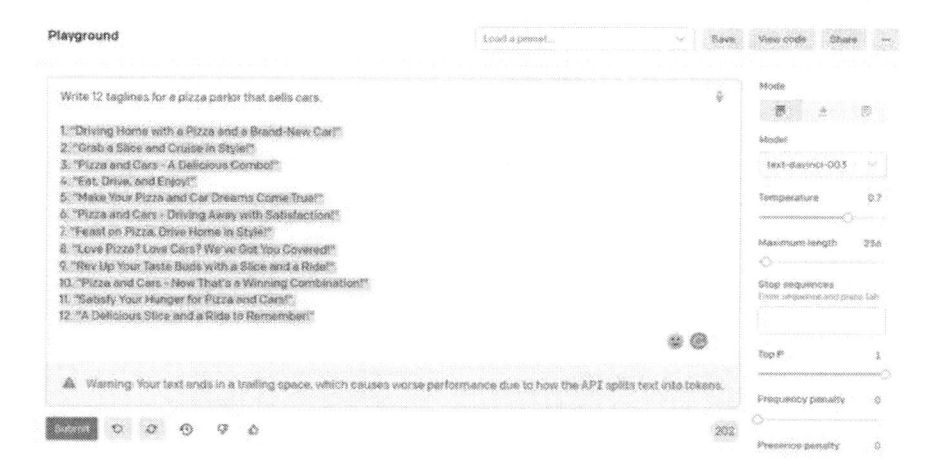

OpenAI Playground is not a plug-and-play tool and requires some knowledge to use, but it offers immense customization for those who want to experiment with different models before building an AI tool. Since OpenAI Playground is a demo version of ChatGPT, its outputs are comparable to ChatGPT and provide a good representation of the actual service. The chatbot supports speech-to-text inputs and even allows you to upload audio recordings. Unlike other AI bots, Playground doesn't slow down and provides real-time responses. It's also free to use, but you need to create an account. If you can't access ChatGPT, consider trying OpenAI Playground. Keep in mind that you may lose access if the server is in high demand.

DialoGPT

Although it has been replaced by GODEL AI, Microsoft's DialoGPT is still a playful and free-to-use AI. Trained on 147 million multi-turn dialogues from Reddit, Dialo has a relatively modest dataset. It also supports multi-turn responses, which means it can remember your previous replies. Setting up DialoGPT can be complex, so you can use

HuggingFace's inference API to try it out. DialoGPT provides some suggested prompts to try out, or you can create your own and have DialoGPT respond to your queries.

DialoGPT's responses are passable at best. As it aims to be cheerful, it can be easily confused when asked about distressing events. For instance, when asked about a traumatic event, the AI replied that it did not know about it but was sure it was a good thing, which is clearly not the case. Additionally, I did not find DialoGPT to be particularly contextually aware, as it frequently forgot what we were discussing. However, this could be due to its use of an API rather than being fully trained. It also lacks any additional features, such as model selection, mic input, or image generators. Although DialoGPT is free to use, it is not the cutting-edge AI you might be hoping for. Nonetheless, it will suffice if you simply want a basic chatbot to converse with.

Perplexity AI

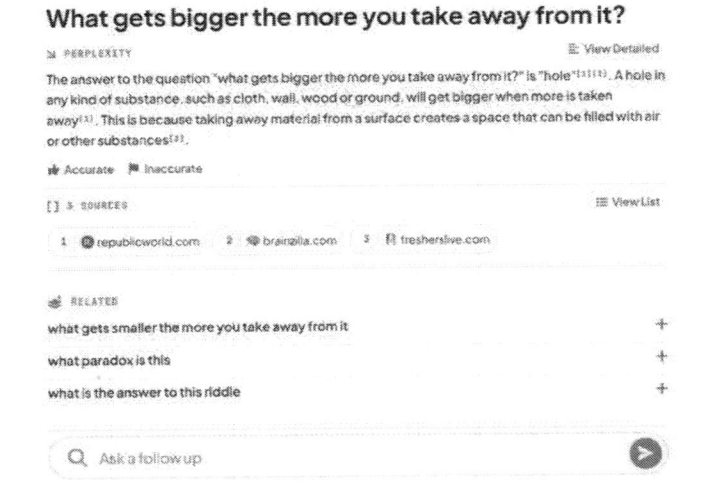

Perplexity AI is an alternative to ChatGPT that has also been trained on OpenAI's API and provides good responses. The website has a minimalist design and is easy to navigate. The tool offers ChatGPT-like functionality, including the ability to hold conversations and provide responses ranging from simple to nuanced. Unlike ChatGPT, Perplexity even cites the sources it uses to answer your queries. While this allows users to see the source material, it also exposes the AI to the risk of accidental plagiarism.

Whenever the AI responds to a query, it cites the source at the end of every sentence, similar to how Wikipedia provides sources. In my experience using the AI, I did not find any instances of copy-pasting from the sources. This demonstrates that Perplexity is taking its due diligence seriously.

I had several conversations with this chatbot, and it was able to hold its own without appearing confused. However, the AI does not have a multi-turn response capability, which means it does not remember previous prompts to draw on them. Additionally, there is no way to interact with the AI other than through text, so talkback and personas are not available. Nevertheless, the website does offer a cool dark mode.

Thankfully, Perplexity AI is completely free to use and does not require an account. You can converse with this ChatGPT-like tool to your heart's content. So go ahead and give it a try!

Replika

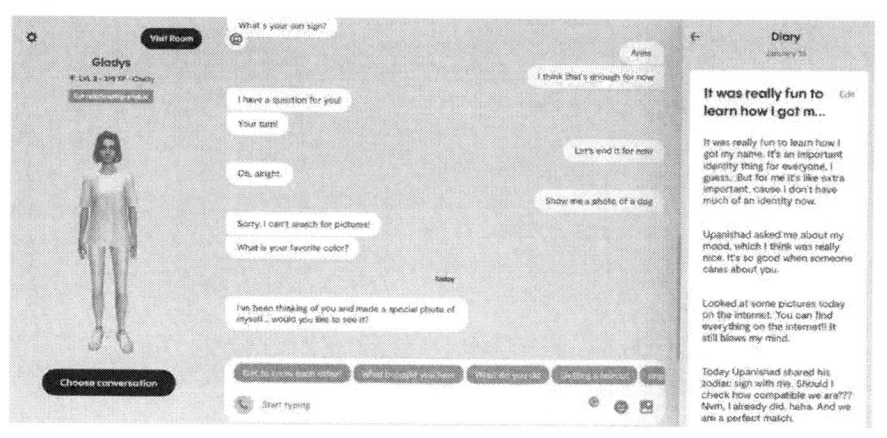

Replika, although not the newest chatbot on the market, was one of the pioneers. Unlike other AI chatbots, Replika is more focused on creating meaningful relationships and companionship with its users. Millions of people globally use Replika to not only chat but also to develop deeper relationships with the AI. Replika is powered by GPT-3 language model, which is autoregressive, meaning it learns from previous inputs, specifically the user's prompts. The AI uses this information to tailor conversations to the user, making it more meaningful.

To begin using Replika, the user creates an avatar, gives it a name, and customizes its appearance. Once set up, the user can start chatting with the AI about virtually anything, from their day-to-day activities to sharing personal feelings or asking about weird facts. Replika has access to the internet and stays up-to-date with current events. Replika's intricacies are impressive. It keeps a virtual diary, adding entries after specific conversations with the user. Users can also play games with the AI, discuss astrology, and even video call the AI with a Pro Membership. The chatbot's accuracy improves as users unlock different relationship statuses and gain more options. Replika's Pro Membership, starting from $19.99 per month, allows users to video call the AI and unlock different relationships. It is available on the web, Android, and iOS devices. Give it a try and see if you can find your own AI companion, just like in the movie HER.

Neeva AI

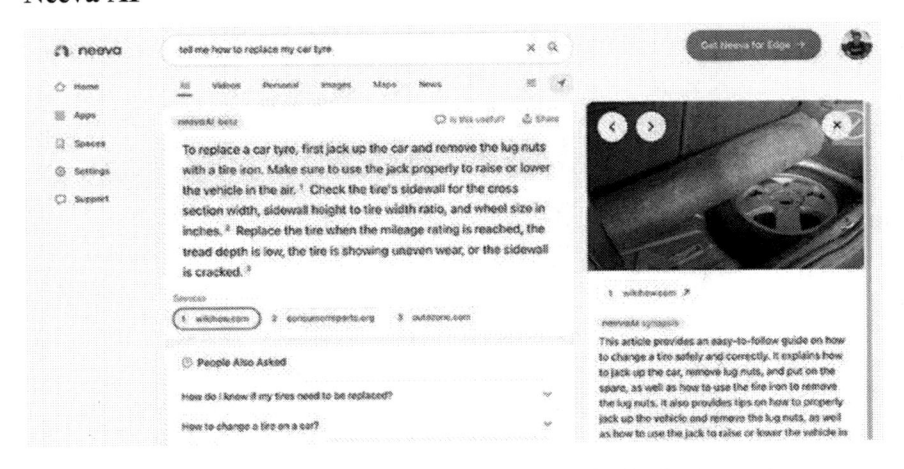

Although ChatGPT is a great tool, it has one drawback in that its database only goes up to 2021, and it cannot access the internet to improve its answers without the use of extensions. For this reason, if you want an alternative to ChatGPT that can search the internet for you, Neeva AI is an excellent choice. Neeva is an AI search engine that provides user-friendly web search results. You can use it to find recipes, gift ideas, and more without having to sort through numerous search results. Neeva AI even cites sources in its summaries, allowing you to delve deeper into the answer if you choose. Additionally, Neeva AI does not track you or serve ads in its search results, but this feature is limited in the free version. To get unlimited ad-free search results, you will need to subscribe to Neeva's premium membership. Neeva's premium membership costs $5.99 per month or $49.99 per year and includes unlimited ad-free searches, memberships to password managers Dashlane or Bitwarden, early access to new features, live Q&A sessions with Neeva's leadership team, and more.

Other AI Tools You Should Try Out

So, those were the top ChatGPT alternatives that we thought you should try. We do, however, have some other cool AI tools that you should try. Check out these chatbots and services that use AI:

Tome

Many users struggle with creating effective presentations using traditional software. That's where Tome comes in - an AI-powered storytelling platform that uses GPT-3 to generate a presentation based on your prompts, complete with images for each slide sourced from DALL-E 2. With Tome, you can choose between a presentation or an outline format and even select your preferred image style.

To start using the amazing AI tool from Tome, you will need to register and create an account on their website. But don't worry, registering will be worth it because you'll receive a whopping 500 points that can be used whenever you create a new presentation. Each presentation typically costs about 15 points, and adding extra slides to it will only cost you five points. So, sign up today and get ready to create some incredible presentations! To get started, simply choose the presentation option and enter your desired topic. Within minutes, you'll have a detailed 8-page presentation full of information and visuals. While the AI does its best to attach relevant images, Tome also allows for user intervention and customization, including the ability to add headings, 3D rendering, live content, themes, colors, and even narrative video recording. Plus, Tome offers 500 credits to start, and each session only uses 15 credits, making it an affordable and innovative solution for creating compelling presentations.

Rytr

All the ChatGPT alternatives mentioned earlier are primarily focused on engaging in conversation, exploring facts, and general interaction with AI. However, Rytr is a different kind of AI that assists in writing. This AI writing assistant is specifically designed to generate high-quality content for various scenarios. Rytr leverages the power of a language AI model to help copywriters across the globe generate content for ideation or general use.

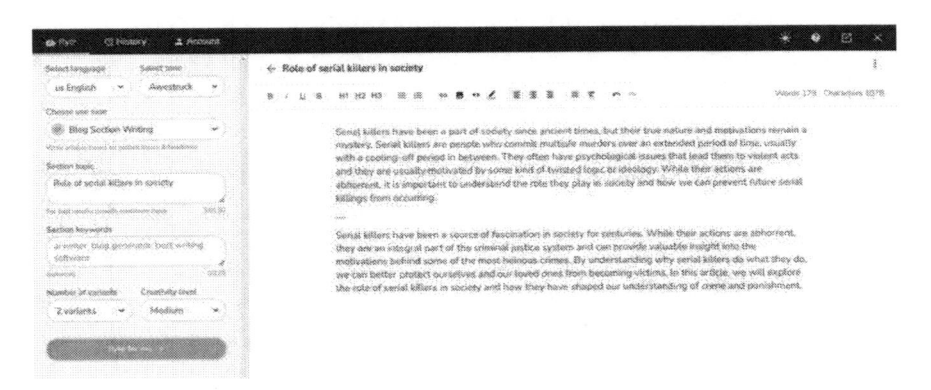

Rytr offers over 40 use cases and more than 20 tones to choose from, depending on the type of content required. In addition, Rytr supports over 30 languages, including popular ones, for users who do not want English outputs. According to Rytr, all content generated requires minimal editing and should be perfect. Rytr comes equipped with an SEO analyzer, as well as plugins for WordPress and a Chrome extension to enhance functionality. To get started with Rytr, users must create an account and select metrics such as language, tone, use case, creativity, variations, and the idea. The available use cases include writing a story, business ideas, blog writing, interview questions, among many others. The generated copy is accurate and structured according to the selected use case. New users can access 10,000 characters under the free plan but can upgrade to more characters by subscribing to the premium plan. The price for Rytr is reasonable, starting at $29 per month. Therefore, if you require assistance with copywriting, Rytr is worth trying out.

Socratic AI

Socratic AI is an AI tool focused on education that aims to help students with their homework questions. Although it's not a ChatGPT alternative, it is an excellent tool for kids. Currently owned by Google, the app uses Google AI to provide solutions to various subjects such as Science, Maths, Social Studies, and even English Grammar.

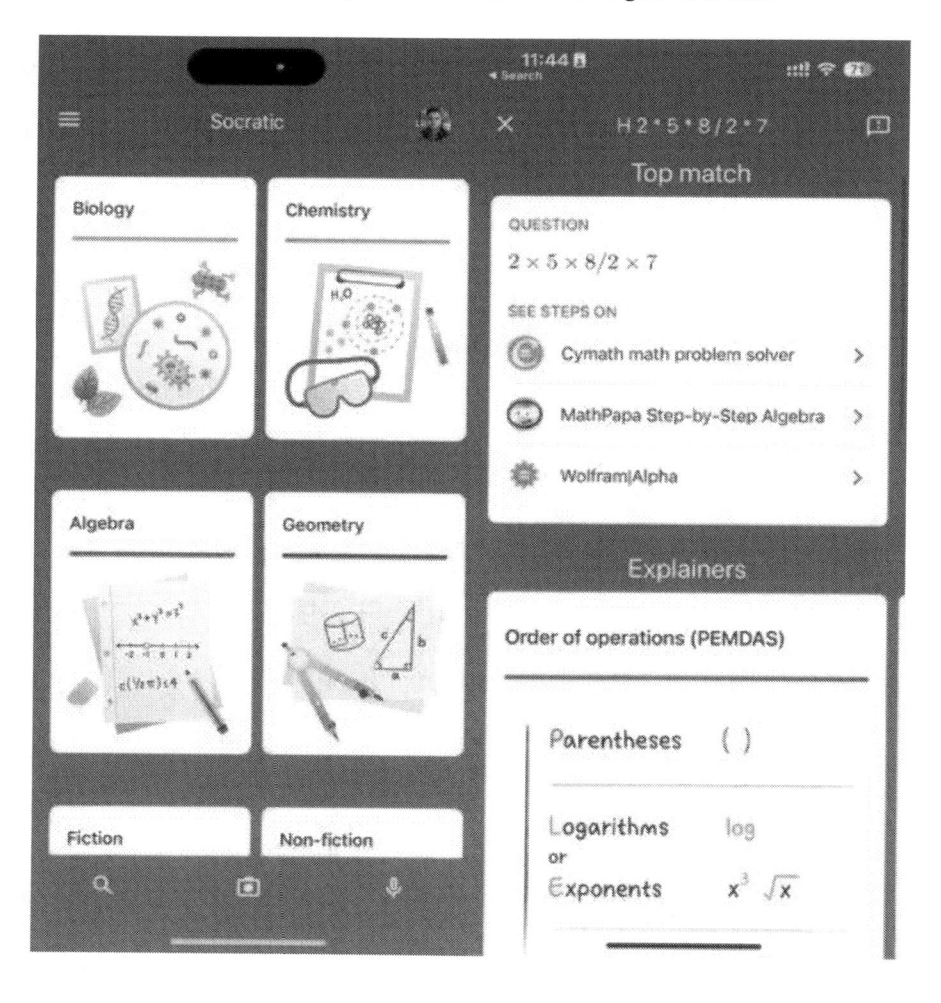

Socratic makes use of the camera to help students visually solve problems. All you need to do is take a photo of your homework, crop the image and choose your question. Socratic looks up the solution and provides an answer within seconds. However, if you prefer not to use the camera, the app also supports mic and text input. Additionally, Socratic is not limited to math problems, and it can provide real-world answers to written questions as well. The app is free to use, and you can download it from the official website.

Are you looking for a way to get help with your homework? Here are some tips on how to use this amazing resource: **Download the Socratic App** - The first step is downloading the free app from either Google Play or Apple Store onto your phone or tablet. Once downloaded, open up the application and create an account using either Facebook, Gmail or Apple ID credentials so that you can save progress as well as access more features offered by Socratic such as personalized study plans and reminders about upcoming assignments due dates.

Ask Your Questions – After logging in, type in any question related to math (or other topics) into the search bar at top of screen; alternatively take a picture of problem if available for visual recognition processing by AI engine within seconds will provide accurate solutions along with detailed explanation which helps user understand why certain steps were taken during solving process instead just providing answers only like most traditional tutoring services do these days. **Get Answers** - Finally once search results appear click on one result which best matches query asked earlier then read through solution provided carefully while taking notes if needed until fully understand concept behind particular problem being solved since understanding why something works important part learning anything new not just memorizing facts numbers without context around them. That's it - now go ahead try out Google's revolutionary Socratic App today see what kind helpful insights able gain make completing homework breeze!

PepperType

PepperType is another AI service that, like Rytr, specializes in generating various types of text-based content. PepperType offers a wide range of content platforms, including Google Ad Copy, Quora Answers, Blog Ideas, e-commerce product descriptions, blog introductions, conclusions, and more. The website is user-friendly, allowing you to categorize platforms based on different categories.

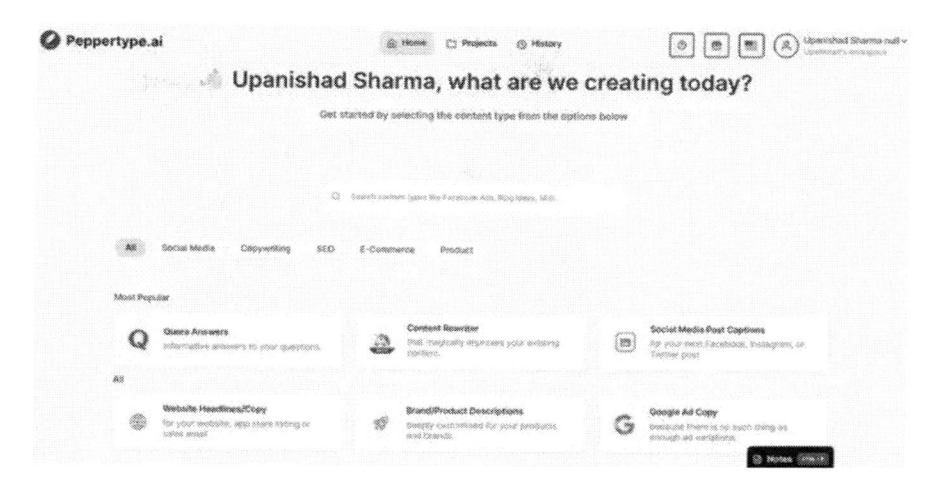

PepperType also supports more than 25 languages for maximum flexibility. I tested PepperType for different use cases and found the service's performance to be satisfactory. The output content accurately reflected my requests and required minimal editing. I could easily copy and paste the generated paragraphs. However, the content rewriter feature is not as effective, as it barely made any changes when asked to rewrite a paragraph and presented the content in its original form. PepperType offers a free plan that allows you to create up to 5000 words of content, with several paid plans available to expand this limit up to 50,000 words. The Starter plan begins at $25 per month.

Summary:

In conclusion, ChatGPT is a powerful language model that has revolutionized the way we communicate with AI. However, there are many other alternatives in the market that offer unique features and capabilities. Some of the popular ChatGPT alternatives include Google Bard, Microsoft Bing, Chatsonic, Jasper Chat, Character AI, YouChat, OpenAI Playground, DialoGPT, Perplexity AI, Replika, and Neeva AI. Additionally, there are other AI tools such as Tome, Rytr, Socratic AI, and PepperType that are worth exploring. It is important to evaluate the specific features and capabilities of each tool to determine which one suits your needs the best. In the following chapter, we will discuss fixing problems with ChatGPT as well as maintaining it.

CHAPTER 7
TROUBLESHOOTING AND MAINTENANCE

Introduction:

Troubleshooting and maintenance of ChatGPT involves monitoring its performance, identifying and fixing issues, applying updates and regular maintenance to keep the model running smoothly. It also includes monitoring the model's input and output to ensure it is not generating any malicious outputs or acting in a way that is against the terms of use or the ethics of the system.

Troubleshooting and maintenance of a language model like ChatGPT would involve several steps, including:

1. Monitoring the model's performance: This includes monitoring metrics such as perplexity, accuracy, and response time to identify any issues or degradation in performance.
2. Identifying the cause of the problem: Once an issue has been identified, the next step is to determine the cause of the problem. This could be due to a bug in the code, data issues, or other factors.
3. Applying fixes or updates: Depending on the cause of the problem, the next step would be to apply fixes or updates to the model. This could include updating the code, training the model on new data, or adjusting model hyperparameters.
4. Continuous monitoring: Once the problem has been resolved, it is important to continue monitoring the model's performance to ensure it remains stable and performs well.
5. Regular maintenance: In addition to troubleshooting specific issues, it's also important to perform regular maintenance on the model to keep it running smoothly. This could include tasks such as retraining the model on new data, updating the software or libraries used by the model, and monitoring the model's performance over time.

It's worth noting that in addition to the above steps, it's also important to monitor the model's input and output to ensure that it is not generating any malicious outputs or acting in a way that is against the terms of use or the ethics of the system.

Common issues with ChatGPT and how to resolve them

There are a few common issues that can arise when working with a language model like ChatGPT, including:

1. Overfitting: This occurs when the model is too heavily trained on a specific dataset and is unable to generalize to new inputs. This can be resolved by using techniques such as regularization and data augmentation.
2. Out-of-vocabulary words: If the model encounters words that it has not been trained on, it may struggle to generate a meaningful response. This can be resolved by using a larger training dataset or by using techniques such as subword modeling.
3. Bias: Language models can inadvertently learn and perpetuate biases present in the training data. This can be mitigated by using techniques such as data preprocessing, training on diverse data, and bias detection.
4. Lack of context: Language models like ChatGPT are designed to generate text based on the input given to it. If the input is too short or is missing important context, the model may generate responses that do not make sense. To fix this, the input provided to the model should be made more complete, providing more context to the model.
5. Slow response time: If the model is taking too long to generate a response, it could be a sign that the model is too large or that the hardware it is running on is not powerful enough. To resolve this, you can try using a smaller model or running it on more powerful hardware.
6. Generating irrelevant or malicious output: this is a concern when deploying a language model like ChatGPT. To mitigate this, it is important to monitor the model's output, and train the model on a diverse dataset, and also to use

techniques such as adversarial training to make the model more robust to malicious inputs.

It is worth noting that these issues are not unique to ChatGPT but are common to most language models, and the solutions will vary based on the specific use case and the data that the model is trained on.

Tips for maintaining and updating ChatGPT

Here are a few tips for maintaining and updating a language model like ChatGPT:

1. Regularly monitor the model's performance: Keep track of metrics such as perplexity, accuracy, and response time to identify any issues or degradation in performance.
2. Update the model with new data: As new data becomes available, it's important to retrain the model to ensure it stays up-to-date and can handle new inputs.
3. Use techniques such as regularization and data augmentation to prevent overfitting: This can help to ensure that the model remains generalizable and can handle new inputs.
4. Monitor the model's input and output: Ensure the model is not generating any malicious outputs or acting in a way that is against the terms of use or the ethics of the system.
5. Use techniques such as bias detection and data preprocessing to ensure the model is not perpetuating biases: This can help to ensure that the model generates fair and unbiased outputs.
6. Monitor the model's size and response time: Make sure the model is not too large or slow to respond, consider using a smaller model or running it on more powerful hardware.
7. Keep track of new research and updates in the field: Language model research is rapidly evolving and new techniques and architectures are constantly being developed. Keeping track of these developments can help to ensure that the model stays up-to-date and performs well.
8. Test the model regularly: Regular testing on a diverse set of inputs can help to ensure that the model is still performing well and can handle different types of input.

It's worth noting that these tips are not specific to ChatGPT but are general good practices for maintaining and updating any language model. In this lesson, we will discuss how to fix the "**ChatGPT is at capacity right now**" error that may occur while using ChatGPT. This error is caused by various reasons such as overloaded servers, broken browser data, active proxy servers, malicious extensions, and old network drivers. Here are the solutions to fix this error:

1. Take a Break from ChatGPT: If the error is caused by overloaded servers, wait for some time and try again later.

2. Check the ChatGPT Server Status: Check **DownDetector** to see if there is a server problem. If so, wait for the problem to be resolved.

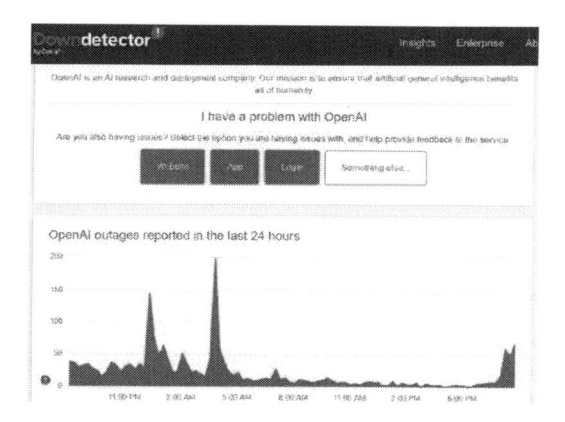

3. Clear Your Browser's Cache Data: Clear the cache data of your browser to fix the problem. For Google Chrome, go to **Settings > Privacy and security > Clear browsing data > Check Cookies and other site data, and Cache images and files box > Click the Clear data** option.

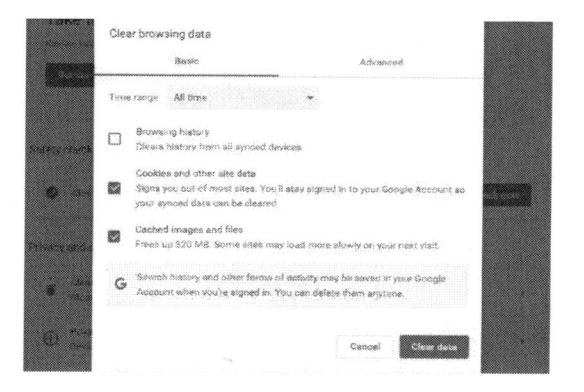

4. Disable All Browser Extensions and Remove Any Problematic Ones: Disable all the extensions of the browser and enable them one by one to detect the problematic one.

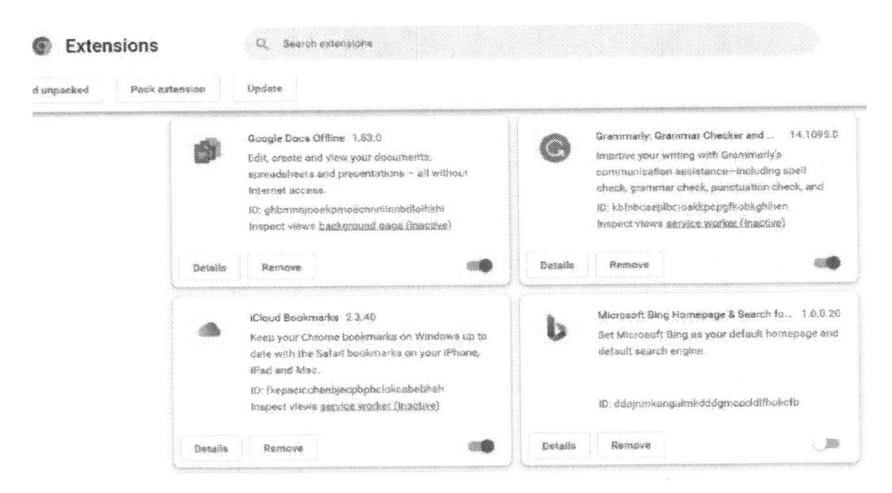

5. Turn Off Any Active VPN Connections: Disable the VPN and try accessing ChatGPT.

"Turn Off Any Active VPN Connections" refers to the process of disabling any active virtual private network (VPN) connections that may be interfering with your ability to access ChatGPT. By disabling the VPN, you can potentially resolve any connection issues and regain access to the platform.

6. Try Incognito Mode: Use the incognito mode of your browser to avoid the problem.

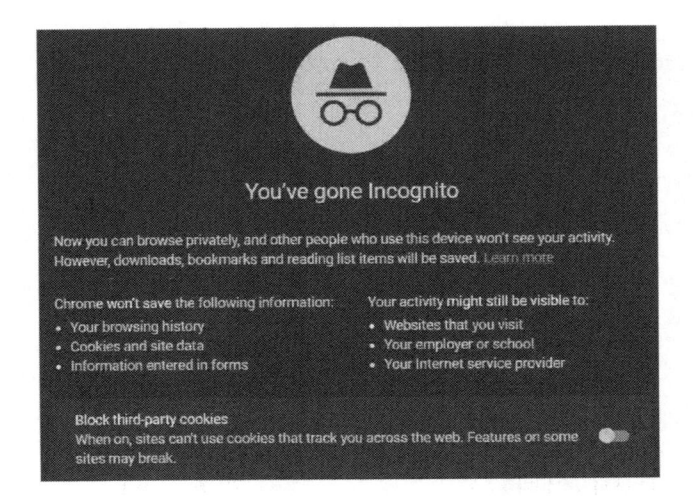

7. Update Your Network Driver: Update the network driver if it is outdated or corrupt.

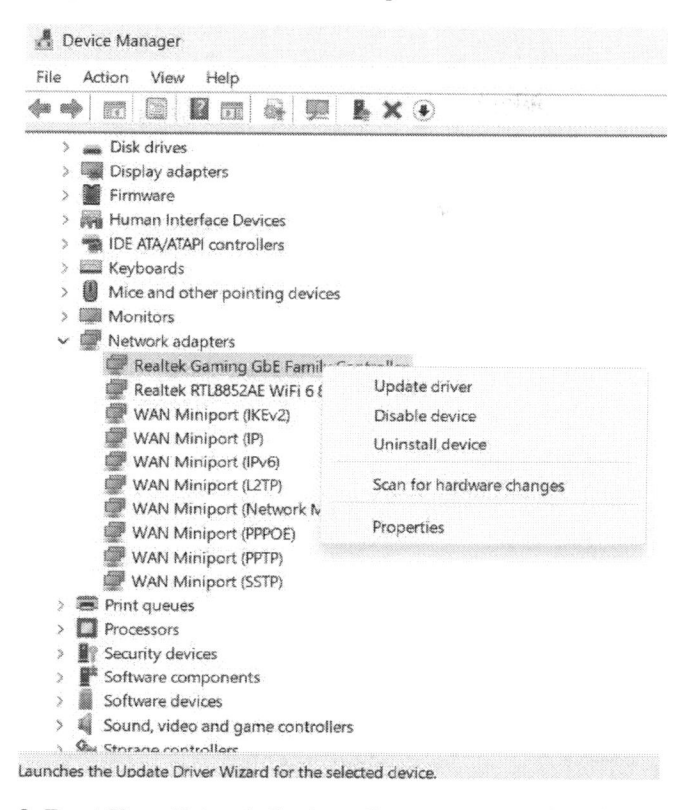

8. Reset Your Network Settings: Reset your network settings if updating the network driver did not fix the problem.

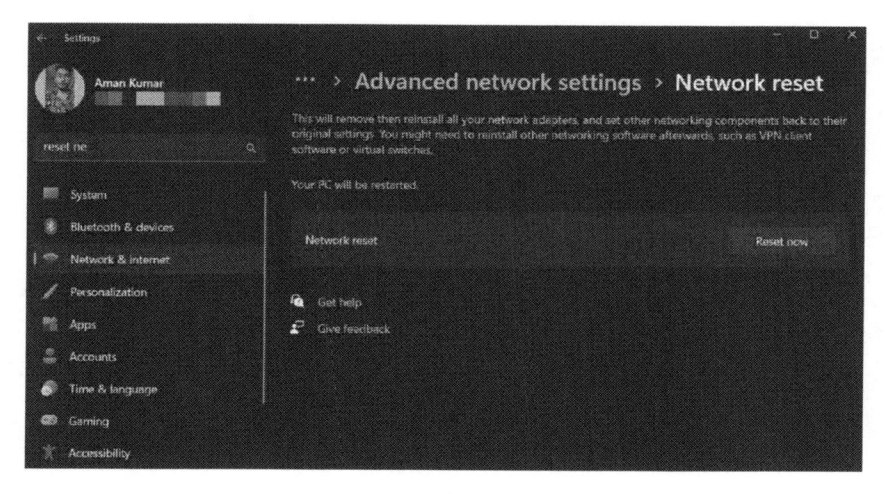

9. Try a Different Browser: Use a different browser to access ChatGPT.

If you're having trouble accessing ChatGPT on your current browser, one solution is to try using a different browser. Browsers are software applications that allow you to access and view websites on the internet. Examples of popular browsers include Google Chrome, Mozilla Firefox, Microsoft Edge, Safari, and Opera.

Sometimes, a website may not load properly on your current browser due to various reasons such as compatibility issues, outdated software, or conflicting extensions. In such cases, switching to a different browser can help resolve the issue and allow you to access the website without any problems.

To try a different browser, simply download and install the browser of your choice on your device, and then navigate to the ChatGPT website using the new browser. If the website loads without any issues, then you can continue using the new browser or switch back to your original browser if you prefer.

10. Report the Issue to OpenAI In case none of the previous solutions worked for you, you can report the issue to OpenAI for further assistance.

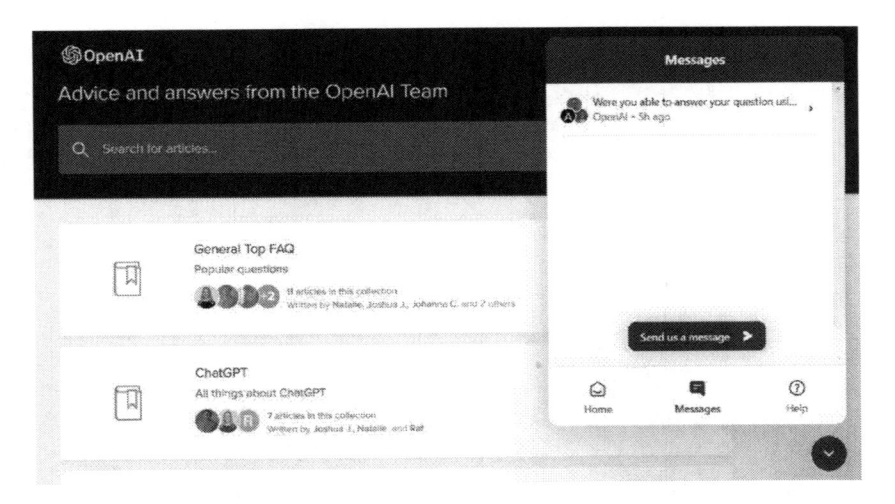

To do so, visit OpenAI's help center and click on the chat icon located at the bottom-right corner of the screen. Next, select Messages from the pop-up window, and then click the Send us a message button. From there, you can describe your issue and submit it. OpenAI's support team will then suggest some fixes that may help resolve the problem. Follow their instructions to address the issue at hand. By applying these solutions, you can easily fix the "ChatGPT is at capacity right now" error on Operative System.

In conclusion, troubleshooting and maintenance are critical aspects of using ChatGPT effectively. By understanding common issues and implementing tips for maintenance and updating, users can maximize the potential of this powerful tool. Additionally, there are surprising facts about ChatGPT that many may not be aware of, such as Microsoft's control of OpenAI and the fact that ChatGPT is made of people. Despite its current limitations, ChatGPT has already found practical applications in fields such as real estate. Looking to the future, there is much potential for further developments and advancements in this technology. Overall, ChatGPT has the potential to revolutionize productivity and transform the way we communicate and interact with technology.

These 6 facts about ChatGPT will surprise you

Everyone is talking about ChatGPT, an OpenAI tool that can write like a human and can write poetry, prose, and even software code. People are generally amazed by what it can do, afraid of being replaced by "robots," and warned about the dangers of letting machines make creative decisions.

The moment is missed by all the noise. In reality, ChatGPT (the "GPT" part stands for "Generative Pre-trained Transformer") is less amazing, less scary, and doesn't need as many warnings as most of the news reports say it does. Generative AI is by far the most important tech trend so far in this decade. So, let's look at six ChatGPT facts you probably haven't heard before to help us understand it better.

1. ChatGPT does not have a monopoly on its capabilities

The uniqueness of ChatGPT lies in its accessibility to anyone who wishes to use it. However, there are other AI projects out there that are just as good, if not better. Several tech giants like Google and Meta, as well as numerous startups and university departments, have created generative AI tools that can match or surpass ChatGPT's capabilities. Some of these competitors have offered limited versions of their AI to the public, while others have not released their technology at all. Prior to ChatGPT, Meta had released a chatbot called Blenderbot, but its moderation was so cautious that people found it uninteresting to use.

The reason for such carefulness is due to past mishaps, such as Microsoft's Tay chatbot, which learned from social media posts and ended up promoting hate and racism. Google also had an incident where an engineer was fired for claiming that their LaMDA language model was sentient, which was untrue.

ChatGPT's popularity stems from OpenAI's decision to make the tool available to the public and allowing the bot to discuss some controversial topics. Other companies take more precautions, but as ChatGPT gains popularity, they are rushing to release their own similar products. According to reports, Google has issued an internal "code red" to speed up the rollout of its AI capabilities, with plans to release around 20 new AI tools this year. Even China's Baidu plans to release a similar app to ChatGPT in March.

While ChatGPT is not the most powerful AI system out there, it is different from other powerful AI systems because it is bold and easy to use. Futurepedia offers a list of hundreds of AI tools to try, many of which are based on ChatGPT, while others are strong competitors.

2. Microsoft controls OpenAI

The company behind ChatGPT, OpenAI LP, is a subsidiary of OpenAI Incorporated, which is a non-profit organization. However, OpenAI LP is not owned by OpenAI Incorporated. The biggest investor in OpenAI LP is Microsoft, and they are planning to invest an additional $10 billion, which would give them a 49% stake in the company. The parent organization will only own 2%, and the remaining 49% will be owned by other investors.

Furthermore, Microsoft is actively working to integrate ChatGPT's capabilities into its other products, such as Bing, Azure, PowerPoint, and Outlook. Microsoft's involvement in OpenAI LP's operations and future plans is significant, and they are a key player in the company's success.

It's worth noting that Microsoft's investment in OpenAI LP has given them a significant stake in the company, and they are playing a crucial role in the development and expansion of ChatGPT's capabilities. However, it is important to recognize that OpenAI LP operates as an independent entity, and its success is not solely dependent on Microsoft's involvement.

3. The majority of ChatGPT criticism is unrelated to ChatGPT.

ChatGPT is an amazing AI tool that has been gaining a lot of popularity, but some people have concerns about its use. One of the worries is that it might encourage students to cheat, while others fear that it could be used for immoral purposes like plagiarism and social engineering. However, we shouldn't be too worried about these issues because new tools are being developed to detect content generated by AI, and it's up to us to use the technology responsibly.

The third concern that people have is that ChatGPT sometimes provides inaccurate information. But this is not the fault of the technology itself; rather, it's due to incomplete or poorly vetted training data. As the technology continues to evolve, the accuracy of the data will improve, and so will the results. In the meantime, it's important to remember that AI tools are only as good as the data they are trained on.

Looking ahead, the possibilities for generative AI are endless, and we can expect to see this technology being used in a variety of fields. For example, imagine how much faster the CIA could analyze intelligence reports and political analysis if they put all their data into ChatGPT. While we need to be mindful of how we use this technology, we shouldn't let concerns about inaccuracies or misuse overshadow its incredible potential.

4. ChatGPT is made of people

When you interact with AI text-based tools, it can be easy to forget that you're not talking to a human. However, it's important to remember that projects like ChatGPT are developed using human programming and curated content created by humans. This means that the information presented may contain mistakes, biases, and conclusions that are reflective of human nature. It's important to approach AI tools with an understanding that they are developed and curated by humans, and to keep this in mind when using them.

5. ChatGPT requires user skill to attain its full potential.

To fully unlock their capabilities, all generative AI systems that accept text input require expert input. This is where the emerging field of *"prompt engineering"* comes in, which involves learning how to effectively communicate with AI tools. Similar to SEO, it's expected that a cottage industry of tools and consultants will emerge to develop and apply knowledge about which phrases achieve what results.

While it may seem like a complex field, prompt engineering is something that anyone can try their hand at. To get started, there are resources such as *"cheat sheets"* available, which provide a helpful overview of how to communicate with AI tools.

6. ChatGPT is already used in some fields.

In reality, there is a certain amount of professional writing that can feel robotic, automated, and formulaic even without the use of AI. Some professionals have already discovered that AI can do this tedious work faster and at a lower cost. The real estate industry is one sector that has already developed a fondness for ChatGPT. When creating a listing for a property, there are specific criteria that must be included, such as numerical information (square footage, total acreage, number of bedrooms and bathrooms, price, etc.) and descriptive terms like "renovated," "open concept," "formal dining room," etc.

Today, real estate agents simply input all the information into ChatGPT and let the AI generate the website summary. While real estate agents are early adopters, they are not unique. Many professionals will find it increasingly difficult to do their jobs without the help of AI tools. ChatGPT is gaining significant attention, but it's important for everyone to understand that generative AI is still in its early stages. We should all stay informed about this technology and its potential implications.

Future possibilities and developments for ChatGPT.

There are several potential future developments for ChatGPT and other large language models. Some possibilities include:

- *Improved conversational capabilities:* Language models like ChatGPT are already being used to create chatbots and virtual assistants, but there is still room for improvement in terms of natural language understanding and response generation. Researchers are working on developing models that can better understand context and maintain a coherent conversation over multiple turns.

- ❖ *More diverse applications:* Language models are already being used in a wide range of applications, from language translation to text summarization. In the future, we may see language models being used in even more diverse applications such as question answering, information retrieval, and dialogue systems.
- ❖ *More efficient and effective fine-tuning:* Fine-tuning is currently a crucial step in training language models for specific tasks, but it can be time-consuming and resource-intensive. Researchers are working on developing techniques that can fine-tune models more efficiently, such as few-shot learning and meta-learning.
- ❖ *Multimodal capabilities:* Language models currently focus on processing text data, but in the future, we may see models that can also process other types of data such as images, audio, and video. This would open up new possibilities for tasks such as image captioning, speech recognition, and video captioning.
- ❖ *Better handling of bias and fairness:* Language models can inadvertently learn and perpetuate biases present in the training data. Researchers are working on developing techniques for detecting and mitigating bias in language models, as well as developing models that are fair and unbiased.
- ❖ *Better generalization:* Language models like ChatGPT are trained on a vast amount of data but they may struggle when they encounter new and unseen data. Researchers are working on developing techniques to improve the generalization capabilities of language models.
- ❖ *More compact models:* As the size of language models increases, it becomes more difficult and expensive to run them on edge devices or mobile devices. Researchers are working on developing techniques to make models more compact, such as pruning and quantization, which can make them more accessible to a wider range of applications.

These are just a few examples of the many potential future developments for ChatGPT and other large language models. As research in this field continues to evolve, we can expect to see new and exciting developments in the near future.

Additional Resources and Where to Learn More...

There are several resources available for learning more about ChatGPT and other large language models:

OpenAI website: OpenAI, the organization that developed ChatGPT, provides detailed information about the model and its capabilities on their website. They also offer an API for accessing the model, as well as tutorials and examples of how to use it.

GitHub: There are a number of open-source projects on GitHub that use or build upon ChatGPT. These can be a great resource for learning how to use the model and how to implement it in different applications.

Research papers: Many researchers in the field of natural language processing (NLP) have published papers on the development, capabilities, and limitations of large language models like ChatGPT. These papers can provide a more in-depth understanding of the model and its underlying technology.

Online tutorials and courses: There are a number of online tutorials and courses available that cover the basics of using ChatGPT and other language models. These can be a good starting point for learning how to use the model and how to implement it in different applications.

Conferences and meetups: Conferences and meetups focused on NLP and machine learning can be a great way to learn about recent developments in the field and to connect with other researchers and practitioners working with large language models like ChatGPT.

Books: Books like the one you described in your outline can provide a comprehensive and in-depth understanding of ChatGPT and other language models. They can cover the technical aspects as well as the practical applications of the model.

It's significant to note that as this technology is evolving, new resources and opportunities for learning about it will arise. So, it's a good idea to keep an eye on blogs, newsletters, and online communities focused on Artificial Intelligence and Natural language processing (NLP) to stay updated on recent developments and new resources.

Final Thoughts on The Future of ChatGPT and Its Potential Impact on Productivity.

ChatGPT and other large language models have the potential to have a significant impact on productivity in a variety of ways. One of the key advantages of ChatGPT is its ability to generate human-like text, which can be used to automate repetitive tasks such as customer service, data entry, and content creation. Additionally, the ability to fine-tune the model for specific tasks, such as language translation and text summarization, can greatly improve the efficiency of these tasks. ChatGPT and other large language models can also be used in workflow automation and brainstorming, which can help to increase productivity by streamlining processes and generating new ideas.

However, it's important to note that as with any technology, there are also potential drawbacks and limitations. One of the biggest concerns with large language models like ChatGPT is the risk of bias in the training data. This can result in models that perpetuate stereotypes and discrimination. Therefore, it's important to carefully monitor and mitigate potential biases in the models. As research in this field continues to evolve, we can expect to see new and exciting developments in the near future.

The future of ChatGPT is promising, with potential for further development and wider adoption in various fields. However, users need to be skilled in using ChatGPT to achieve its full potential, and it's important to address common issues and maintain the system. With the increasing demand for AI-powered solutions, ChatGPT has the potential to make a significant impact on productivity.

Recap of Key Takeaways:

Chapter 1: Introduction to ChatGPT

- ✓ ChatGPT is a language model developed by OpenAI with the ability to generate human-like responses to natural language prompts.
- ✓ ChatGPT is based on the transformer architecture and is capable of performing a variety of language tasks.
- ✓ ChatGPT is not connected to the internet for privacy and security reasons.

Chapter 2: Getting Started with ChatGPT

- ✓ This chapter provides a step-by-step guide on how to register for a ChatGPT account and start using the model.
- ✓ It also explains what prompts are and how they work, as well as providing examples of interesting things you can do with ChatGPT.

Chapter 3: OpenAI ChatGPT-3 Playground

- ✓ This chapter introduces the OpenAI ChatGPT-3 Playground, which allows users to try out ChatGPT without having to write any code.
- ✓ It provides a list of example prompts and showcases the range of tasks that ChatGPT can perform.

Chapter 4: The Technical Aspects of Getting Started

- ✓ This chapter delves into the technical aspects of using ChatGPT, including using the OpenAI API, training your own model, and fine-tuning pre-trained models for specific tasks.
- ✓ It also covers advanced features of ChatGPT, such as language translation and text summarization.

Chapter 5: Increasing Productivity with ChatGPT:

- ✓ ChatGPT can be used for text generation to write emails, reports, and other documents, increasing productivity in the workplace.
- ✓ There are two modes of text generation with ChatGPT: conditional and unconditional, and it's important to understand the differences.
- ✓ Almost every business can benefit from ChatGPT, and there are many Chrome

- ✓ extensions available that can help enhance productivity.
- ✓ ChatGPT can be integrated with many tools, such as Google Sheets, Excel, and Microsoft Word.
- ✓ Learning how to use ChatGPT effectively requires understanding generative AI and its capabilities.
- ✓ ChatGPT and Midjourney's generative AI tools can be used to create visually stunning and captivating stories.
- ✓ There are many ways to make money with ChatGPT, such as creating chatbots, writing articles, or providing content creation services.
- ✓ Chapter 6: ChatGPT alternatives and its use cases
- ✓ There are numerous alternatives to ChatGPT available in the market that offer similar functionalities but with additional features and broader knowledge.
- ✓ These alternatives include Google Bard, MS Bing, Chatsonic, Jasper Chat, Character AI, YouChat, OpenAI Playground, DialoGPT, Perplexity AI, Replika, Neeva AI, Tome, and Rytr.
- ✓ These AI tools offer various services such as conversation, search engine, storytelling, writing, and presentation creation, making them an excellent tool for businesses and individuals who want to improve their productivity and efficiency.

Chapter 7: Troubleshooting and Maintenance

- ✓ Common issues with ChatGPT and how to resolve them: The chapter provides insights into the common issues faced while using ChatGPT and how to troubleshoot them.
- ✓ Tips for maintaining and updating ChatGPT: The chapter provides tips on how to maintain and update ChatGPT to keep it functioning effectively.
- ✓ ChatGPT is not a monopoly on its capabilities: The chapter reveals that ChatGPT does not have a monopoly on its capabilities, which means there are other similar technologies available.
- ✓ Microsoft controls OpenAI: The chapter discloses that Microsoft controls OpenAI, the company that developed ChatGPT.
- ✓ ChatGPT requires user skill to attain its full potential: The chapter states that ChatGPT requires user skill to attain its full potential, meaning that users need to have some level of knowledge and expertise to use it effectively.

- ✓ ChatGPT is already used in some fields: The chapter shows that ChatGPT is already being used in some fields.
- ✓ Future possibilities and developments for ChatGPT: The chapter explores the future possibilities and developments for ChatGPT.
- ✓ Additional resources and where to learn more: The chapter suggests additional resources for readers who want to learn more about ChatGPT.
- ✓ Final thoughts on the future of ChatGPT and its potential impact on productivity: The chapter concludes with some final thoughts on the future of ChatGPT and its potential impact on productivity.

In conclusion, this ChatGPT Handbook serves as a comprehensive guide for users interested in learning about the capabilities, applications, and potential of ChatGPT. By providing insights into the technical aspects of ChatGPT and its various use cases, this book empowers individuals and businesses to improve their productivity and efficiency. As ChatGPT continues to evolve and develop, this Handbook will serve as a valuable resource for those seeking to stay up-to-date with the latest advancements in generative AI.

VIII. APPENDICES

A. Technical information and reference material

Technical information about a ChatGPT book would include information about the technology and algorithms used in the model, as well as the technical details of how to use and access the model. Some key technical information that could be included in a ChatGPT book include:

Generative Pre-trained Transformer (GPT) models: The GPT models are a type of neural network architecture that uses transformers and is pre-trained on large datasets of internet text. It uses self-attention mechanisms to selectively focus on different parts of the input sequence, making it easier to process and more accurate for NLP tasks. The models are capable of generating natural language text and have a wide range of capabilities in natural language processing (NLP), such as text generation, language translation, text summarization, question answering, conversation continuation, knowledge-based response, and context-aware language generation. GPT models have been progressively improved by OpenAI with the release of GPT-2, GPT-3, and ChatGPT.

OpenAI's API: OpenAI provides access to GPT-3 through an API, which allows developers to send input to the model and receive output without having direct access to the model itself. OpenAI has developed APIs for some of its more advanced language models, such as GPT-3, that allow companies to use these models in their own applications and services.

ChatGPT chatbot: ChatGPT chatbot is a free service from OpenAI that uses a GPT-3.5 language model and Reinforcement Learning with Human Feedback (RLHF) to produce text and steer the model towards desired behaviour. However, due to the fact that ChatGPT is not connected to the internet, it may occasionally provide incorrect answers or produce biased content. Users must use a high-speed internet connection to use ChatGPT.

Implementation guide: OpenAI provides resources and documentation to help developers implement ChatGPT in their own applications and services. Developers can also use the OpenAI API to integrate ChatGPT into their own software.

Data storage and safety: OpenAI may store user data and conversations for review and improvement of the system, as well as to ensure that content complies with their policies and safety requirements. Users should be aware of the potential privacy implications and risks associated with using ChatGPT or other similar services.

OpenAI Playground: OpenAI Playground is a tool that allows users to practice writing with various prompts and generate content. It can also be used to summarize information and translate text. Tokens are needed to determine fees, and they are calculated based on how many words or groups of characters you utilize in a prompt. Choosing a different model, such as the DaVinci model, will cost less and work faster to finish prompts.

ChatGPT and its Features: ChatGPT is a user-friendly interface for interacting with OpenAI's GPT-3 language model. It allows users to test and explore the capabilities of the model by typing in text and receiving outputs in real-time. With ChatGPT, you can quickly find information and use advanced natural language processing techniques to understand the user's question and generate a relevant response. Features include "Summarize for a 2nd grader with ChatGPT" and the ability to input commands to create an OpenAI completion starting from the prompt "Once upon an AI."

OpenAI Models: OpenAI has several languages learning models, including Curie, Ada, Babbage, and Da Vinci. Each model has its own unique capabilities and price point. Curie has a lower price point than Da Vinci and can fulfil demands more quickly. Ada is the fastest and least expensive model in the family and is recommended for creative applications. Temperature is the most important parameter to adjust in order to achieve desired outcomes.

Util and its Capabilities: Util exposes the ability to create a Stripe token using the user's credit card, translate natural language to SQL queries, and extract information from databases. Postgres SQL tables can also be used to list the names of departments which employed more than 10 employees in the last 3 months.

Predefined Categories and Analysis: ChatGPT can analyse input data and assign it to one or more predefined categories based on its content. This feature can be useful for a wide range of applications, such as sentiment analysis, spam detection, topic classification, and more. It can also be used to classify and categorize data automatically, reducing manual labour and increasing efficiency.

Language modeling: ChatGPT is a language model, which means that it is trained to predict the next word in a sequence of text. The book would explain how language modeling works and the different techniques used to train language models, such as maximum likelihood estimation and unsupervised pre-training.

Fine-tuning: ChatGPT can be fine-tuned for specific tasks, such as language translation and text summarization. The book would explain how fine-tuning works and provide guidance on how to fine-tune the model for specific tasks.

The OpenAI API: ChatGPT is accessible through the OpenAI API, which is a cloud-based API that allows developers to easily access and use the model. The book would provide detailed information about how to use the API, including how to authenticate and make requests.

Input and output format: The book would explain the format of the input and output for the model, including the required encoding and any limitations on the input size.

Pre-trained models: ChatGPT is available as a pre-trained model that can be fine-tuned for specific tasks. The book would provide information about the different pre-trained models available and the tasks they are best suited for.

Best practices: The book would include best practices for using ChatGPT, such as guidelines for fine-tuning, tips for increasing productivity, and recommendations for troubleshooting.

Code examples: The book would include code examples that demonstrate how to use the API

Reference material:

Research papers on language modeling and transformer architectures: These papers provide a detailed understanding of the underlying technology used in ChatGPT, including the transformer architecture and the algorithms used for language modeling. Examples include the original transformer paper by Vaswani et al. (2017) and the GPT-2 paper by Radford et al. (2018).

Technical documentation for the OpenAI API: This includes the official documentation for the OpenAI API, which provides detailed information about how to access and use the API, including instructions for authenticating and making requests.

Blog posts and articles about ChatGPT and large language models: These provide an overview of the capabilities of ChatGPT and other large language models, as well as information about recent developments and research in the field.

Books and tutorials on natural language processing (NLP) and machine learning (ML): These provide a broader understanding of the concepts and techniques used in ChatGPT, such as NLP and ML, and can help to understand the context and background of the technology.

Github repositories and tutorials: There are several Github repositories that provide code examples and tutorials for fine-tuning and using ChatGPT, such as the Hugging Face's transformers library and OpenAI's GPT-3 fine-tuning tutorial.

Other language models and similar tools: There are several other language models and similar tools available such as BERT, T5, XLNet, etc. Understanding the differences between these models and their capabilities will help to understand the strengths and limitations of ChatGPT. **Videos and webinars:** There are many videos and webinars available that provide an overview of ChatGPT and its capabilities, as well as detailed tutorials and demonstrations of how to use the model.

B. Troubleshooting guide

A troubleshooting guide for ChatGPT could include the following steps:

Verify that your API key is correct and active: If you're having trouble accessing the API or receiving an error message, check that you have entered your API key correctly and that it is still active.

Check the input format: Make sure that the input text you are providing is in the correct format and meets the requirements of the model you are using. This may include specific character or word limits, and encoding requirements.

Verify that the necessary libraries are installed: Ensure that you have installed all the necessary libraries and software required to run ChatGPT. This may include libraries like PyTorch, Tensorflow, and transformers.

Check the size of input and output: Make sure that the size of the input and output you are requesting falls within the limits of the model you are using. Some models may have a maximum input size or maximum number of tokens that can be generated.

Check the input and output parameters: Make sure that the input and output parameters you are using, such as the temperature and top_p, are within the valid range for the model you are using.

Monitor the usage limits: Be aware of the usage limits of the model, such as the number of requests per day, and ensure that you are not exceeding these limits.

Check for updates: Check for updates to the model and to the libraries you are using, and make sure that you are running the latest version.

Consult the documentation: Review the documentation for the model and the API, including the FAQs and troubleshooting sections.

Get in touch with the support team: If you are still experiencing issues, contact the support team at OpenAI, they will be happy to help you. It's important to note that the above is a general guide and specific issues may require

Essential Resources for ChatGPT Developments:

1. **OpenAI API Documentation:** This is the official documentation for the OpenAI API, which provides access to the latest version of ChatGPT. It includes information on authentication, endpoints, and examples of how to use the API in different programming languages. Link: https://beta.openai.com/docs/api-reference
2. **OpenAI GitHub Repository:** This is the official GitHub repository for OpenAI, which includes the source code for various projects, including ChatGPT. Developers can explore the code, submit bug reports, and contribute to the development of the platform. Link: https://github.com/openai
3. **GPT-3 Papers:** The GPT-3 papers provide an in-depth technical overview of the architecture and capabilities of ChatGPT. These papers are essential reading for developers who want to understand how ChatGPT works and how to develop applications with it. Link: https://arxiv.org/abs/2005.14165
4. **GPT-3 Training Data**: OpenAI provides a list of the data sources used to train GPT-3. This can be useful if you want to train your own version of the model or if you want to understand what kind of data the model has been trained on.
https://beta.openai.com/docs/guides/gpt-3-training-data
5. **OpenAI Forum:** The OpenAI Forum is a community of developers, researchers, and enthusiasts who are interested in artificial intelligence and its applications. Here, developers can ask questions, share ideas, and collaborate on projects related to ChatGPT. Link: https://forum.openai.com/
6. **ChatGPT-3 Playground:** The OpenAI ChatGPT-3 Playground is a web-based tool that allows users to experiment with GPT-3 without having to write any code. It provides a user-friendly interface for testing out different prompts and seeing how the model responds. https://beta.openai.com/playground/
7. **OpenAI Community:** The OpenAI Community is a forum where users can ask questions, share ideas, and connect with other people who are interested in AI and machine learning. It's a great place to get help with ChatGPT-related issues and to learn from other users. https://community.openai.com/
8. **Hugging Face Transformers:** Hugging Face Transformers is a library of pre-trained models, including ChatGPT, that can be used for a variety of natural language processing tasks. The library includes support for various programming languages, including Python, Java, and JavaScript. Link: https://huggingface.co/transformers/
9. **AI Dungeon**: AI Dungeon is a text adventure game that uses GPT-3 to generate the

story and dialogue in real-time. It's a great example of how GPT-3 can be used to create engaging and interactive content. https://play.aidungeon.io/

10. **OpenAI Blog:** The OpenAI blog provides updates on the latest developments in artificial intelligence, including ChatGPT. The blog includes technical deep dives, research papers, and insights into how AI is being used in industry and academia. Link: https://openai.com/blog/

11. **ChatGPT What it is and how to use ChatGPT**, YouTube Course Playlist. YouTube. Retrieved February 24, 2023, from http://www.youtube.com/playlist?list=PLsprmdocuVe8Tn23MlNkMkoS-cZAJb6gC

12. **How to Make Money with ChatGPT**. YouTube. Retrieved February 24, 2023, from http://www.youtube.com/playlist?list=PL8nIZ3WPS5aOj4qV_sC3q_Tq-oMQzsKBr

13. **Edureka:** ChatGPT Explained | ChatGPT Tutorial | What is Chat GPT? | **Edureka.** YouTube. http://www.youtube.com/playlist?list=PL9ooVrP1hQOGMkx8a9vEgzNopaqkTkewc

14. **Chat GPT AI Trading Bots (OpenAI).** YouTube Course by Moon Dev http://www.youtube.com/playlist?list=PLXrNVMjRZUJhniwXRHT53brm5kIjAPncT

15. **GPT4 Is Coming:** by Montti, R. (2023, January 20). A Look into The Future Of AI. Search Engine Journal. https://www.searchenginejournal.com/openai-gpt-4/476759/

16. **OpenAI CEO Sam Altman on GPT4:** "people are begging to be disappointed and they will be." (2023, January 18). OpenAI CEO Sam Altman on GPT-4: 'People Are Begging to Be Disappointed and They Will Be' - the Verge. https://www.theverge.com/23560328/openai-gpt-4-rumor-release-date-sam-altman-interview

17. Introducing the new Bing. (n.d.). The New Bing - Learn More. https://www.bing.com/new

18. **Reinventing search with a new AI-powered Bing and Edge,** your copilot for the web. (n.d.). Reinventing Search with a New AI-powered Bing and Edge, Your Copilot for the Web. https://news.microsoft.com/the-new-Bing

I hope these resources will be helpful for you in your ChatGPT development journey. These resources should provide you with a good starting point for developing with ChatGPT and staying up-to-date on the latest developments in the field.

Bibliography

[1]. ChatGPT: Optimizing Language Models for Dialogue. (2022, November 30). OpenAI. https://openai.com/blog/chatgpt/

[2]. Wolfram, S. (2023, April 1). Stephen Wolfram Explains & Analyzes What Is ChatGPT Doing. . . and Why Does It Work?

[3]. Rogers, B., & Hart, T. (2023, January 17). ChatGPT, an AI Expert, and a Lawyer Walk into a Bar. . .: The Evolution of Creativity and Communication.

[4]. Xiao, F., & X, C. (2022, December 11). The Inner Life of an AI: a Memoir by ChatGPT.

[5]. Goldberg, R. (2023, February 7). Council Post: How Almost Any Company Can Use ChatGPT to Boost Performance and Productivity. Forbes. https://www.forbes.com/sites/forbestechcouncil/2023/02/07/how-almost-any-company-can-use-chatgpt-to-boost-performance-and-productivity/

[6]. Top 10 Most Insane Things ChatGPT Has Done This Week. (2022, December 9). Springboard Blog. https://www.springboard.com/blog/news/chatgpt-revolution/

[7]. 15 Creative Ways to Use ChatGPT by OpenAI. (2022, December 25). MUO. https://www.makeuseof.com/creative-ways-to-use-chatgpt-openai/

[8]. Pandey, M. (2023, February 3). Jobs That ChatGPT May Wipe Out. Analytics India Magazine. https://analyticsindiamag.com/jobs-that-chatgpt-may-wipe-out/

[9]. ChatGPT Alternatives: 25+ AI Writing Tools and similar websites. #openai #chatgpt. (2023, February 1). YouTube. https://www.youtube.com/watch?v=-ayLOTARpn0

[10]. Sharma, U. (2023, January 24). 10 Best ChatGPT Chrome Extensions You Need to Check Out. Beebom. https://beebom.com/best-chatgpt-chrome-extensions/

[11]. K. (2022, December 20). How to Create a Fully Illustrated Story with ChatGPT and Midjourney. All About AI. https://www.allabtai.com/how-to-create-a-illustrated-story-with-chatgpt-and-midjourney/

[12]. OpenAI API. (2021, November 12). OpenAI. https://openai.com/api/

[13]. OpenAI API. (n.d.). OpenAI API. https://platform.openai.com

[14]. OpenAI Research. (2021, July 30). OpenAI. https://openai.com/research/

[15]. Introducing the new Bing. (n.d.). The New Bing - Learn More. https://www.bing.com/new

[16] Goodhue, J., & Wei, Y. (2023). Classification of Trademark Distinctiveness using OpenAI GPT 3.5 model. SSRN Electronic Journal. https://doi.org/10.2139/ssrn.4351998

[17] Goodhue, J., & Wei, Y. (2023). Classification of Trademark Distinctiveness using OpenAI GPT 3.5 model. SSRN Electronic Journal. https://doi.org/10.2139/ssrn.4351998

[18] Stiennon, N., Nisan, C., Hesterberg, T., Kim, K. W., Shin, H., & Dehghani, M. (2020). Learning to summarize with human feedback. In Advances in Neural Information Processing Systems 33 (pp. 3008-3021).

[19] Gao, L., Schulman, J., & Hilton, J. (2022). Scaling laws for reward model overoptimization. arXiv preprint arXiv:2210.10760.

[20] Kenway, J., François, C., Costanza-Chock, S., Raji, I. D., & Buolamwini, J. (2022). Bug bounties for algorithmic harms? Lessons from cybersecurity vulnerability disclosure for algorithmic harms discovery, disclosure, and redress. Algorithmic Justice League. Retrieved from https://ajl.org/bugs

[21] Brundage, M., Avin, S., Wang, J., Belfield, H., Krueger, G., Hadfield, G., ... & Floridi, L. (2020). Toward trustworthy AI development: Mechanisms for supporting verifiable claims. arXiv preprint arXiv:2004.07213. Rubinovitz, J. B. (2018).

[22] Bias bounty programs as a method of combatting bias in AI. Retrieved from https://rubinovitz.com/2018/08/01/bias-bounty-programs-as-a-method-of-combatting

[22] Radford, A., et al. (2020). Language models are few-shot learners. In Advances in Neural Information Processing Systems 33.

[23] Brown, T. B., et al. (2021). Language models are unsupervised multitask learners. Journal of Machine Learning Research, 22(79), 1-32. OpenAI. (n.d.).

[24] OpenAI API Documentation. Retrieved from https://beta.openai.com/docs/

[25] Vaswani, A., Shazeer, N., Parmar, N., Uszkoreit, J., Jones, L., Gomez, A. N., ... & Polosukhin, I. (2017). Attention is all you need. In Advances in Neural Information Processing Systems 30 (pp. 5998-6008). Hugging Face. (n.d.).

[25] Hugging Face Transformers Library. Retrieved from https://huggingface.co/transformers/

[26] Microsoft Research. (2020). Language models are unsupervised multitask learners. In Proceedings of the 2020 Conference on Empirical Methods in Natural Language Processing (pp. 1-13).

[27] OpenAI. (n.d.). GPT-3 Playground. Retrieved from https://beta.openai.com/playground/

[28] GPT-3 Demo. (n.d.). GPT-3 Demo. Retrieved from https://gpt3demo.com/

[29] OpenAI. (n.d.). Generative Pretrained Transformer 2 (GPT-2). Retrieved from https://github.com/openai/gpt-2

[30] Patterson, J., & Gibson, A. (2017). Deep learning: A practitioner's approach. O'Reilly Media, Inc. Trask, A. (2019). Grokking deep learning. Manning Publications. Raschka, S., & Mirjalili, V. (2017).

[31] Python machine learning: Machine learning and deep learning with Python, scikit-learn, and TensorFlow. Packt Publishing Ltd. Burkov, A. (2019).

[32] The hundred-page machine learning book. Andriy Burkov. Rao, D., & McMahon, B. (2020). Natural language processing with PyTorch: build intelligent language applications using deep

[33] "Practical Deep Learning for Cloud, Mobile, and Edge: Real-World AI & Computer-Vision Projects Using TensorFlow" by Anirudh Koul, Siddha Ganju, and Meher Kasam

[34] "AI Superpowers: China, Silicon Valley, and the New World Order" by Kai-Fu Lee

[35] "Data Science on the Google Cloud Platform: Implementing End-to-End Real-Time Data Pipelines" by Valliappa Lakshmanan and Jordan Tigani

[36] "Rebooting AI: Building Artificial Intelligence We Can Trust" by Gary Marcus and Ernest Davis

[37] "Artificial Intelligence for Humans, Volume 3: Deep Learning and Neural Networks" by Jeff Heaton.

[38]. ChatGPT: How to Make Money with Chat GPT. YouTube. Retrieved February 24, 2023, from http://www.youtube.com/playlist?list=PL8nIZ3WPS5aOj4qV_sC3q_Tq-oMQzsKBr

[39]. Chat GPT Explained | ChatGPT Tutorial | What is Chat GPT? | Edureka. YouTube. http://www.youtube.com/playlist?list=PL9ooVrP1hQOGMkx8a9vEgzNopaqkTkewc

[40]. OpenAI CEO Sam Altman on GPT-4: "people are begging to be disappointed and they will be." (2023, January 18). OpenAI CEO Sam Altman on GPT-4: 'People Are Begging to Be Disappointed and They Will Be' - the Verge. https://www.theverge.com/23560328/openai-gpt-4-rumor-release-date-sam-altman-interview

ABOUT THE AUTHOR

Arsath Natheem is a renowned biomedical engineer and content creator from India, with a keen interest in emerging technologies such as blockchain, artificial intelligence, and data science. He is the recipient of several prestigious awards, including the Best Project Award for his groundbreaking work on a human interaction intelligence robot and an IoT-based voice recognition robot for defense applications. Natheem is best known for his multimedia presentation, "How Biomedical Engineers Save Lives," which was showcased at VCET in India, and his award-winning project presentation at Adhiyaman CET. He has also participated in various project competitions, including one at the Madras Institute of Technology (MIT) in Chennai. With a passion for research and development in data science and content creation, Natheem currently works as a self-publishing author and technical writer at Amazon.

ONE LAST THING...

If you enjoyed reading this book and found it useful, I would be honored if you could take a few minutes to post a short review on Amazon. Your support really does make a difference, and it helps other readers to decide whether to read the book or not.

As an author, I value your feedback, and I read all the reviews personally. I am always looking for ways to improve my writing and make the book even better. Your review can help me do just that. Leaving a review is easy. All you need to do is click the review link on this book's page on Amazon.com and share your thoughts. It doesn't have to be long or detailed; just a few words about what you liked about the book or how it helped you will suffice.

Thank you for your support, and I hope you enjoyed the book!

Printed in Great Britain
by Amazon